Maths and Non-verbal Reasoning

Assessment Practice for the **CEM** test

Ages 10–11+ Year 6

Alison Primrose

Great Clarendon Street, Oxford OX2 6DP

Oxford University Press is a department of the University of Oxford. It furthers the University's objective of excellence in research, scholarship, and education by publishing worldwide. Oxford is a registered trade mark of Oxford University Press in the UK and in certain other countries

Text © Alison Primrose 2023
Illustrations © Oxford University Press 2023

The moral rights of the authors have been asserted

All rights reserved. No part of this publication may be reproduced, stored in a retrieval system, or transmitted, in any form or by any means, without the prior permission in writing of Oxford University Press, or as expressly permitted by law, by licence or under terms agreed with the appropriate reprographics rights organization. Enquiries concerning reproduction outside the scope of the above should be sent to the Rights Department, Oxford University Press, at the address above.

You must not circulate this work in any other form and you must impose this same condition on any acquirer

British Library Cataloguing in Publication Data
Data available

978-0-19-277984-7

10 9 8 7 6 5 4 3 2 1

Paper used in the production of this book is a natural, recyclable product made from wood grown in sustainable forests. The manufacturing process conforms to the environmental regulations of the country of origin.

Printed in China

Acknowledgements

Content Development Adviser: Michellejoy Hughes
Content Development Adviser and Reviewer: Jane Cooney
Additional material by Michellejoy Hughes
Page make-up: Integra Software Services
Cover illustrations: Lo Cole
Illustrations: Integra Software Services and Tech-Set Ltd, Gateshead

Although we have made every effort to trace and contact all copyright holders before publication this has not been possible in all cases. If notified, the publisher will rectify any errors or omissions at the earliest opportunity.

Contents

Welcome 4
A Note for Parents 5
How to Use This Book 6

Learning Papers

Special Numbers, Place Value and Sequences ... 8
Logic and Shapes 13
Number Skills and Grids 18
Transformations, Ratios and Proportions 23
Algebra and Codes 27
Measurement 31
Geometry and Nets 34
Statistics 39
Curveball Questions 1:
Logic, Symmetry and Number Skills 48

Mixed Papers

Mixed Paper 1 50
Mixed Paper 2 56
Mixed Paper 3 61
Mixed Paper 4 66
Curveball Questions 2:
Logic, Sequences and Codes 71

Test Papers

Test Paper 1 72
Test Paper 2 80

Keywords 92
11+ Study Guide 94
Answers A1
Progress Chart A18

Two further Mixed Papers are available online at **www.bond11plus.co.uk**

Welcome

The CEM Select Entrance Assessment is a computer-based 11+ test that assesses a child in verbal, non-verbal and mathematical reasoning. It covers English and maths topics that a child will be familiar with from the National Curriculum, but, in common with other 11+ exams, supplements these with verbal reasoning and non-verbal reasoning questions. What makes the CEM exam different from other assessments is the way that it blends English and verbal reasoning in one test and then maths and non-verbal reasoning in another, rather than offering four separate tests. CEM (Centre for Evaluation and Monitoring) do not offer their own practice materials or past papers and deliberately vary the contents of the exam each year, which means that the CEM 11+ is often seen as being more challenging to prepare for.

All Bond 11+ materials are effective preparation for CEM Select and develop the skills and aptitudes that a child needs for success, but CEM-specific titles, like this one, are designed to hone the flexibility of approach essential to overcoming the particular challenges of the CEM test. The Bond system provides learning, information and consolidation so that children have an extended, rich education. Our aim is to familiarise children with the type of questions they will find in the exam and to give them the transferable skills that will allow a child to attempt any question in any exam.

Bond offers a complete, flexible programme of preparation materials that you can adapt to your child's specific needs and to the requirements of the exam, or exams. There are timings provided for each section. Children can complete a paper in one sitting, using the overall timings, or in smaller sections. The CEM online exam has an additional 25% time allowance for candidates needing additional support. If this applies to your child, add an extra 25% for each timed section.

Why Use a Book to Prepare for an Online Test?

Since 2022, the CEM Select 11+ test has only been offered as a computer-based assessment. Whilst it is worth spending some test-practice time using an online platform such as Bond Online to gain familiarity with completing assessments through a digital interface, books remain a highly effective way of developing the skills necessary for success in a structured way whilst reducing screen time.

Not Just for the CEM Select 11+

This book has been designed to be especially effective preparation for the rigours of the CEM 11+ test, but the skills can be applied to any 11+ exams or independent school entrance exams and are also great for engaged pupils looking for an extra challenge or to ready themselves for secondary school.

Remember to keep checking in with your school of choice so that you know which exam they use – schools do change their exam boards from time to time. If your exam board does change, all is not lost. This book will still have been good preparation for other exam boards.

KEY STUDY SKILLS

Working towards an entrance exam can be an exciting challenge. It is the chance to learn new things and to prepare for secondary school. Here are some tips to help you:

- Create a study schedule so that you have a regular routine

- Balance short bursts of practice with longer assessment papers

- Create a quiet study space with pencils, an eraser, paper for working out, your books and a notebook for copying strategies in. If you study in different places, keep everything in a box that you can take with you

- Write down strategies to solve new topics, but don't forget to revise and consolidate

- Limit distractions such as television, technology and games when you are studying

- Remember that errors are useful. They are part of the journey to success.

A Note for Parents

Parents have a crucial role in helping children and motivating them. Here are some ways that you can really make a difference.

- Check your child is working at the right level. The goal is being able to score 85% on average. It's demotivating if they can't complete questions. It is also important that they work through the system so that they are at the right level for the exam at the right time

- Mark work promptly and go through errors. If papers have not been marked, a child has no idea how they are doing or whether they are repeating the same mistake

- Use the Bond Handbooks to help your child understand new techniques

- Limit the range of homework you give your child. The best results are achieved by a system that gradually increases in difficulty. Completing lots of books and papers doesn't guarantee your child's success and often creates stress

- If your child is struggling with something specific, add additional support in that area. If your child is not achieving an 85% average in CEM-specific books you can also use other subject-specific Bond Assessment Practice books at the same level or Bond 10 Minute Tests for consolidation

- Communication is key. Remain positive and encourage your child to focus on the positive. No exam is going to ask for 100% so pushing for that is unrealistic and stressful

- If your child is constantly struggling, be realistic over whether a selective education is the right choice for your child now. Many children move to a selective school for their GCSEs or A levels so not going to a selective school now doesn't mean they never will. It is about finding the best school for your child.

How to Use This Book

This book includes many step-by-step techniques for solving different question types. If further support is needed it can be used alongside one or more of the Bond Handbooks, which offer insights into the full range of questions that might occur in the exam.

- The first section of the book is the Learning Papers that focus on key skills with worked examples then lots of questions for consolidation.

- The second section of the book is Mixed Papers so that children continue to consolidate and do not forget what they have learnt. Go online at **www.bond11plus.co.uk** and register for free resources to get two additional Mixed Papers.

- The final section includes two full Test Papers, which can be broken down into shorter sections for more focussed practice, or can be used as full mock tests for that all-important exam practice.

- There is an 11+ study guide at the back of the book with some useful hints and tips.

- There are fully worked out answers to explain how an answer has been reached.

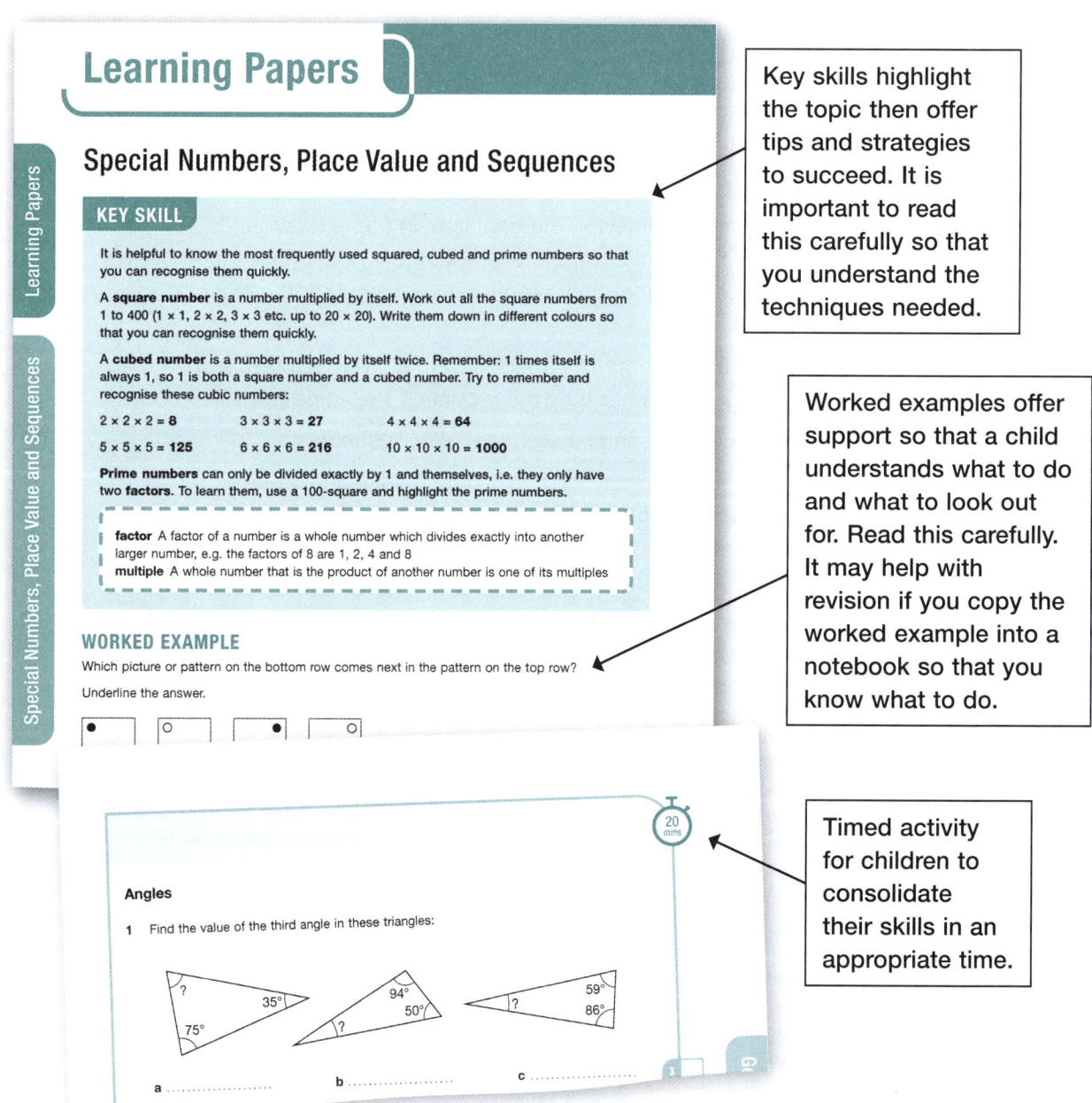

Key skills highlight the topic then offer tips and strategies to succeed. It is important to read this carefully so that you understand the techniques needed.

Worked examples offer support so that a child understands what to do and what to look out for. Read this carefully. It may help with revision if you copy the worked example into a notebook so that you know what to do.

Timed activity for children to consolidate their skills in an appropriate time.

KEY MATHS AND NON-VERBAL REASONING SKILLS

The Bond Maths and Non-Verbal Reasoning Book covers the elements that are found in the CEM online 11+ exam, but is useful for all CEM-style online and written 11+ exams. The Learning Papers cover the following key skills:

- **Mathematics** – a wide range of topics including data, arithmetic and problem solving
- **NVR** – including rotational, reflection, series, sequences and similarities
- **Spatial** – including cubes/nets, 2D and 3D shapes, transformations, and shape combinations.

The Mixed Papers ensure the key skills are consolidated thoroughly then the Test Papers give children the opportunity to get used to the exam process as a natural progression of each book. Don't forget that a rounded education is key. Get used to reading graphs, timetables and charts. Try doing Sudoku and number games, play online games like Tetris or Snake and have a go at some logic and number puzzles – Bond has a number of puzzle books to help make this more fun. Create an ongoing list of strategies or techniques such as 'how to find volume' or 'how to multiply with decimals' to extend your maths skills.

Each book is part of the Bond system with books increasing gradually in difficulty. Once your child has completed this book, there is a clear progression in starting the next book level if your child has an average of 85% in this book. If they have achieved an average of 70% – 85%, then another book at the same level as this one will provide further support. If your child has achieved less than a 70% average, then moving down a level will be most useful. Once your child has developed the skills needed at a lower level, they can move up with confidence.

Learning Papers

Special Numbers, Place Value and Sequences

KEY SKILL

It is helpful to know the most frequently used squared, cubed and prime numbers so that you can recognise them quickly.

A **square number** is a number multiplied by itself. Work out all the square numbers from 1 to 400 (1 × 1, 2 × 2, 3 × 3 etc. up to 20 × 20). Write them down in different colours so that you can recognise them quickly.

A **cubed number** is a number multiplied by itself twice. Remember: 1 times itself is always 1, so 1 is both a square number and a cubed number. Try to remember and recognise these cubic numbers:

2 × 2 × 2 = **8**   3 × 3 × 3 = **27**   4 × 4 × 4 = **64**

5 × 5 × 5 = **125**   6 × 6 × 6 = **216**   10 × 10 × 10 = **1000**

Prime numbers can only be divided exactly by 1 and themselves, i.e. they only have two **factors**. To learn them, use a 100-square and highlight the prime numbers.

> **factor** A factor of a number is a whole number which divides exactly into another larger number, e.g. the factors of 8 are 1, 2, 4 and 8
> **multiple** A whole number that is the product of another number is one of its multiples

WORKED EXAMPLE

Which picture or pattern on the bottom row comes next in the pattern on the top row? Underline the answer.

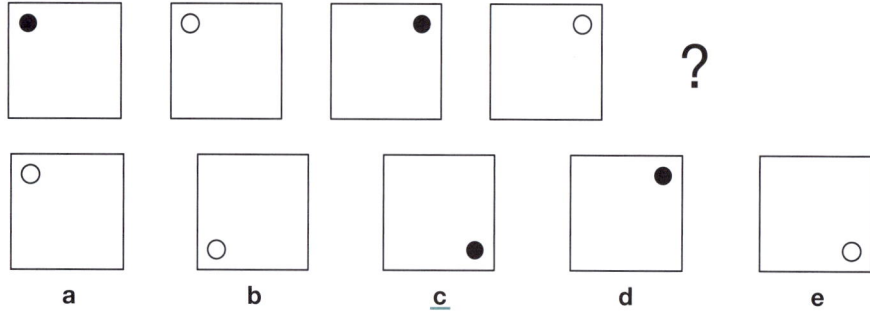

Look at the top row. The circles alternate between black and white. The position of the circles in the squares could be a repeating pattern, such that there are two in the top left corner, then two in the top right corner, so the next one might be in the top left again. Or it could be that the circles are moving around the corners of the square in a clockwise direction, so the next two would be in the bottom right. This is the case here, as the correct answer is **c**.

When it seems that there are two possible answers look at the answer options given to identify which is correct. If you think that two answers are possible, select the one that is the best fit.

NVR Sequences and Analogies

Which picture or pattern on the bottom row comes next in the pattern on the top row? Underline the answer.

1

a   b   c   d   e

2

a   b   c   d   e

3

a   b   c   d   e

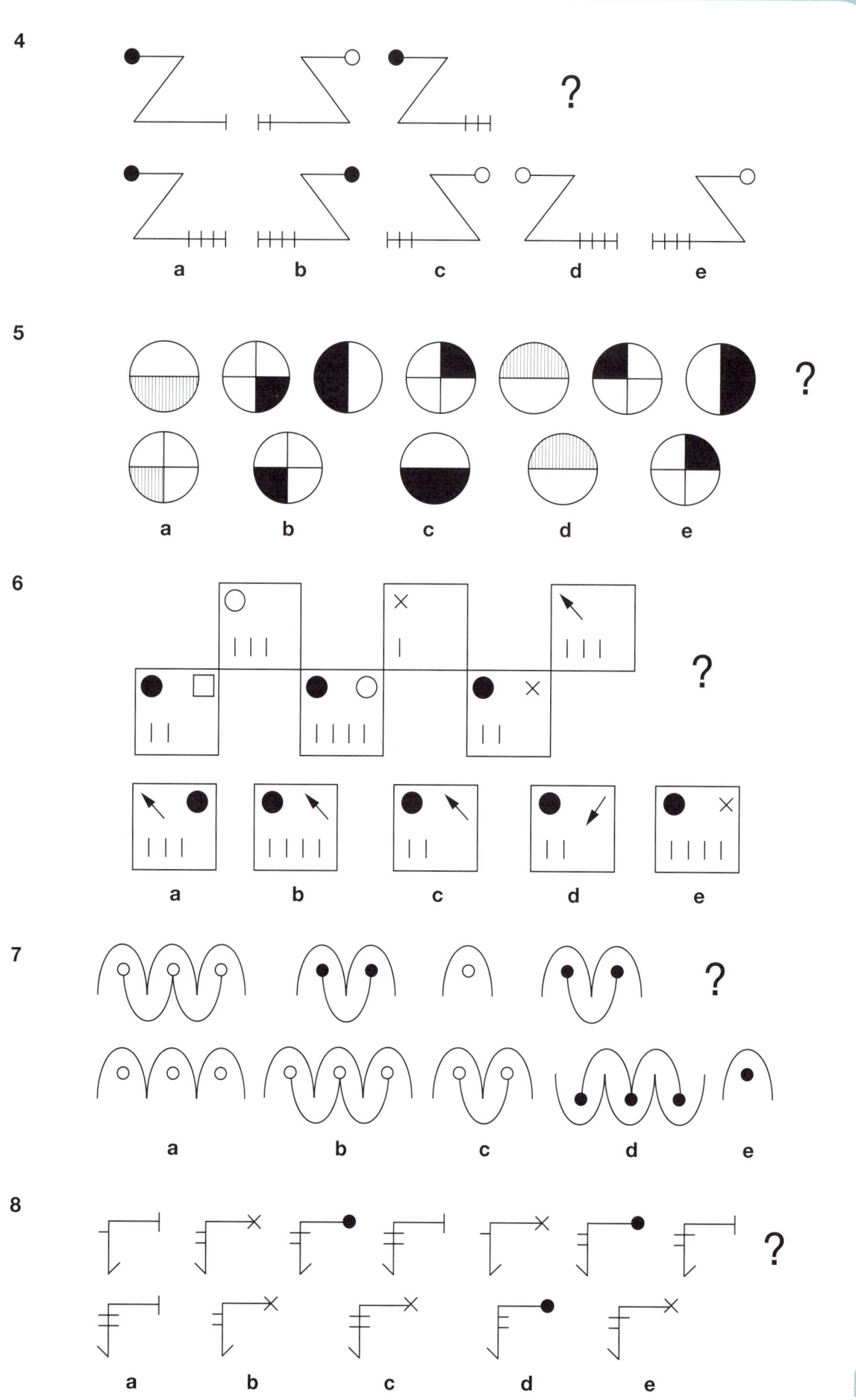

Place Value

9 $10^2 \times 0.0319 \times 10^3 =$ ....

10 .... $\times 2000 = 220\,000$

11 Write in words the total of $50\,002 + 300\,100$ ....

12 Find the **total** of all the digits in the hundreds and the tenths columns of these three numbers:

    1505.66   9191.119   11 367.482   ....

13 What number is two thousand and two less than ten thousand?
Write your answer in numbers.

....

14 Complete the following table, the first one has been done for you.

	× 10	× 1000	÷ 10	÷ 100
3.4	34			
16.78				
4750				

15 Round 7948.852

    a to the nearest tenth ....

    b to the nearest whole number ....

    c to the nearest ten ....

    d to the nearest hundred ....

> **TOP TIP!**
> When **rounding** to a specific decimal place remember to write the zero. For example, 8.9 rounded to one decimal place is 9.0

16 Complete this number chain:

$100 \times 10^2 =$ .... $\div 1000 =$ .... $\times 10^3 =$ ....

Number Types

17 Which of the following numbers is a **multiple** of 3, 4 and 5?

   222   240   445   280   453   ....

18 Which of these numbers have 4 and 7 as **factors**?

   49   56   700   160   210   168   ....

19 The temperature falls 13 degrees from 6°C in the day. What is the night temperature?

   ....

> **TOP TIP!**
> A symbol that looks like a small circle (°) is often used after the digit when showing degrees instead of writing the word 'degrees'

20 What is the sum of the **prime** numbers between 20 and 30?

   ....

21 One night the temperature fell to –11°C. It went up 13 degrees during the day but then fell 4 degrees the next night. What was the temperature on the second night?

   ....

22 Underline the **cube** numbers:

   125   216   333   525   900   1000

23 Give three more pairs of **factors** for 42:

   1 and 42, ...

24 Give a number less than 100 which has 2, 3, 4 and 5 as **factors**.

   ....

Total 28

Logic and Shapes

KEY SKILL

Logic questions provide some information and then ask for that information to be applied to a different pattern or problem. To solve these problems the given information has to be inspected very carefully.

- If dealing with a word problem, it can help to write down or highlight the key pieces of information
- If it is a problem with shapes, look for elements such as the number of shapes or number of sides, or their shading, size or angles
- When answer options are given, it can help to cross out answers that can be eliminated as you work through the question.

WORKED EXAMPLES

Which is the odd one out? Underline the answer.

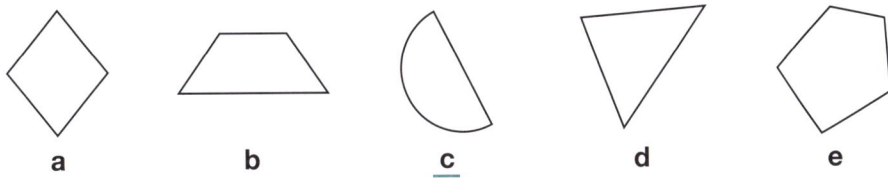

Do all but one of the shapes have the same number of sides? **No, there are several differences in the number of sides.**

Is there any variation in the shading? **No, they are all the same.**

Do all but one of the shapes have straight lines? **Yes, a, b, d and e all have straight lines and no curved lines. C has both straight and curved lines, so c is the odd one out.**

Which shape or pattern on the right belongs to the group on the left? Underline the answer.

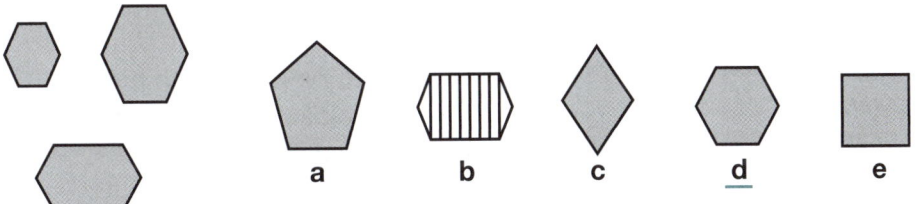

Do all the shapes on the left have the same number of sides? **Yes, they all have six sides.**

Is there any variation of shading? **No, they are all the same.**

Look at the answer options, is there another shape with six sides and the same shading? **Yes, option d.**

13

NVR Similar and Different Shapes

Which is the odd one out? Underline the answer.

1

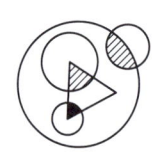    

    a   b   c   d   e

2

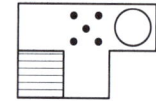 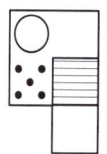 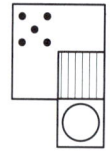 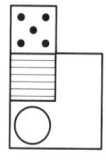 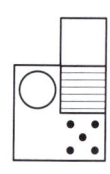

    a   b   c   d   e

3

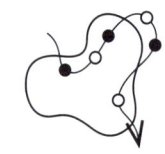   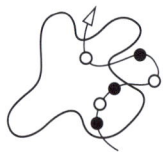 

    a   b   c   d   e

4

  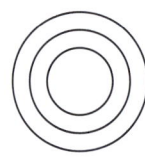  

    a   b   c   d   e

Which shape or pattern on the right belongs to the group on the left? Underline the answer.

TOP TIP!

If there appears to be more than one option, look very closely at the detail and choose the best fit

5

                            a   b   c   d   e

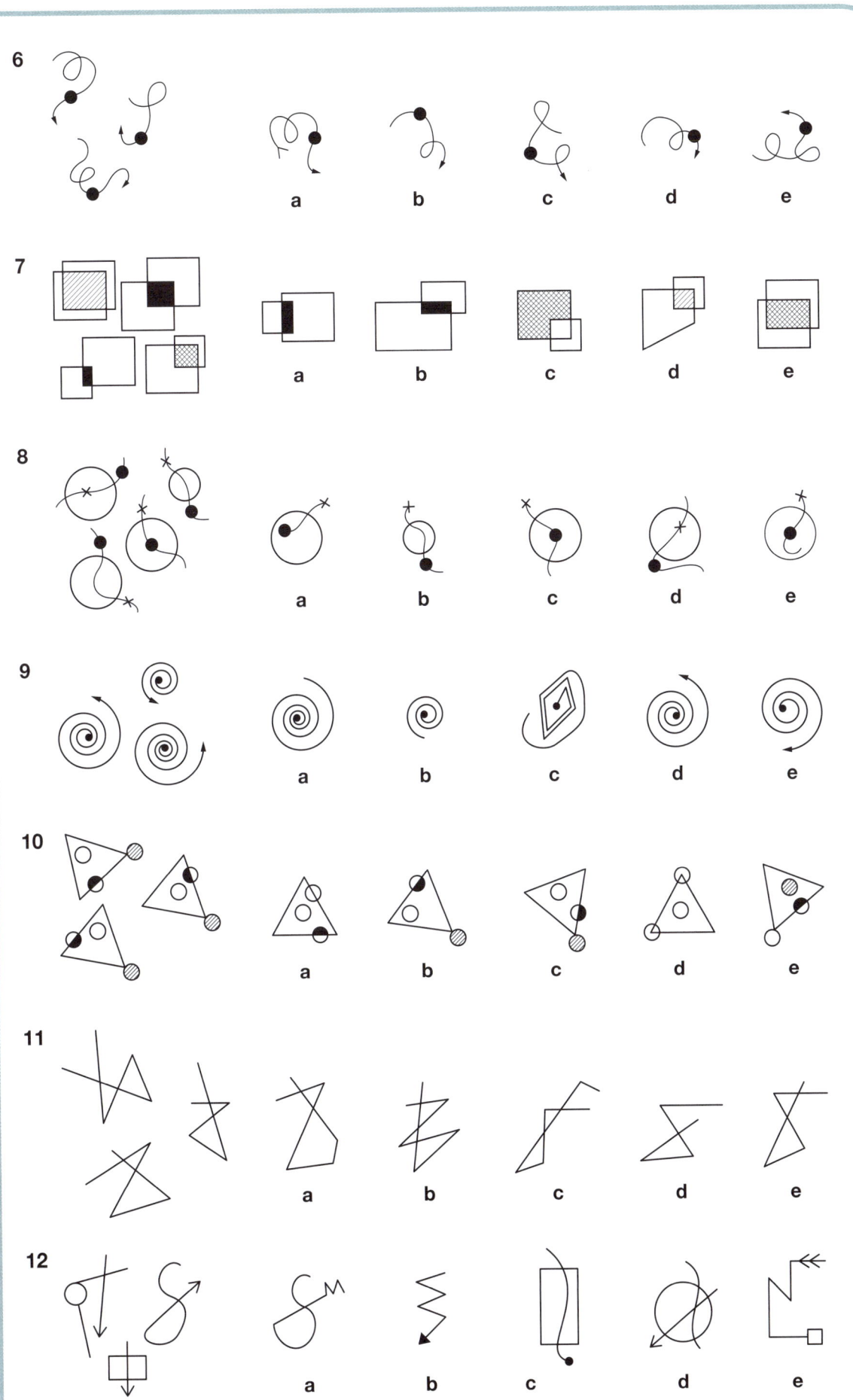

Word and Logic Problems

13 A new library is being set up to house 3000 books. A shelf length of 30 cm is allowed for 10 books. What is the minimum amount of shelving required for all of the books? Give your answer in metres.

> **TOP TIP!**
> When tackling word problems, either write short statements about the facts you are given, or draw a simple diagram, which is especially helpful if the question involves directions, angles or sequencing

....

14 A class of 20 children go to the theatre. Group tickets at the theatre are £40 for 5 people. The coach for the trip costs £280. If the cost is shared equally among the children, how much must they each pay?

....

15 Insert the numbers 1 to 9 in this grid so that each column and each row adds up to 15. Each number should be used only once.

16 100 raffle tickets are sold, numbered 1 to 100. The winning ticket is an odd number. It is a multiple of 3. It is greater than 20. It is a multiple of 5. It is less than 66. What is the winning number?

....

17 Ben is three years older than his sister and a third of the age of his mother. His father is four years older than his mother and four times the age of his sister. How old is Ben?

....

16

18 A street has **even** house numbers starting with number 2 at the end by the main road. The sixth and seventh house along the street have been taken down to make a park, but the other numbers have not been changed.

Andrea lives at number 26 and her friend lives eight houses away nearer the main road. What house number does her friend live at? ....

19 This diagram shows the distances in kilometres between a number of different villages.

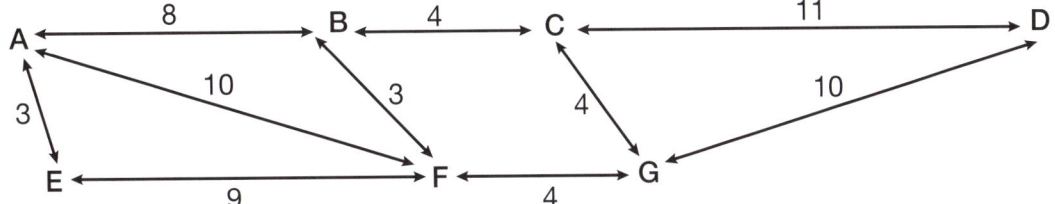

a What is the shortest distance from village G to village A? ....

b How many kilometres are covered travelling the shortest way from village D to E, through villages C and F? ....

c Through which village/villages will a walker pass doing a 16 km walk from village A to G? ....

20 There are twice as many red beads as blue beads in a box.
There are 20 more blue beads than green beads.
There are three times as many yellow beads as green beads.
If there are 15 yellow beads, how many beads are red?

....

21 A water tank containing 300 litres of water has a leak, losing 1 litre of water every 8 hours. After how many weeks and days will the tank be half empty?

....

22 Taz is five years older than his brother and one year younger than his cousin.
His uncle is three times the age of his cousin and four times the age of his brother.
How old is Taz?

....

Number Skills and Grids

> ### KEY SKILL
>
> **Working with fractions**
>
> Fractions can be simplified when both the top number (the numerator) and the bottom number (the denominator) can be divided exactly by the same whole number.
>
> If they cannot be divided by the same number then the fraction is in its simplest form.
>
> E.g. $\frac{3}{6}$ Both numbers can be divided exactly by 3 giving $\frac{1}{3}$
>
> $\frac{7}{10}$ There are no numbers that divide exactly into 7 and 10, so this is in its simplest form
>
> The denominator, or bottom number in a fraction, shows you how many parts the whole has been divided into.
>
> The numerator, or top number of a fraction, shows you how many of the equal-sized parts of the whole are being considered.
>
> To find a fraction equivalent to another fraction, multiply the numerator and the denominator by the same number.
>
> When adding or subtracting fractions, all of the fractions need to have the same denominator, then the numerators are simply added or subtracted according to the calculation required.
>
> When multiplying fractions, the numerators are multiplied and the denominators are multiplied.
>
> An improper fraction is one that has a value greater than one, i.e. the numerator is bigger than the denominator. Improper fractions can also be written as mixed numbers,
>
> e.g. $\frac{7}{4} = 1\frac{3}{4}$
>
> **Working with decimals**
>
> When calculating with decimal numbers, remember to keep the decimal point in line when doing addition or subtraction calculations. With multiplication of decimal numbers, carry out the sum without any decimal points, then add together the number of decimal places in the two numbers being multiplied and insert the point to give that same number of decimal places in the answer.

WORKED EXAMPLES

Adding fractions:

$\frac{2}{5} + \frac{3}{4} = \frac{8}{20} + \frac{15}{20} = \frac{23}{20} = 1\frac{13}{20}$ An improper fraction can be simplified and given as a mixed number

Change these fractions so that they have the same denominator which will be the lowest common **multiple**, which for 4 and 5 is 20

Multiplying fractions:

$\frac{3}{4} \times \frac{1}{2}$ Numerators 3 × 1 gives 1, denominators 4 × 2 gives 8, so the answer is $\frac{3}{8}$

Note that the multiplication sign can be read as 'of' so $\frac{3}{4}$ of $\frac{1}{2}$ is the same as $\frac{3}{4} \times \frac{1}{2}$.
It is asking for a fraction of another fraction, so the answer will be less than one.

Multiplying decimals:

51.73 × 6.5 =

	5	1	7	3	
	×	6	5		
3	1	0	3	8	0
	2	5	8	6	5
3	3	6	2	4	5

Round (*can be to the simplest number rather than the nearest number*) and estimate 50 × 7 = 350, and the answer will have 3 decimal places

Decimal point goes here giving **336.245**

Check – is 336 close to 350?
Yes, so the decimal point is in the correct place

Fractions

1 $\dfrac{\left(\frac{1}{2} \times 620\right)}{2}$ = ...

2 Fill in the missing number: $5\frac{1}{2} -$ .... $= 2\frac{3}{4}$

TOP TIP!
A horizontal line in an equation as in question 1 means divide

3 A string of flags is made up of red, blue, green and orange flags. Half of the flags are blue, and one-tenth are orange. There is an equal number of red flags and green flags. If there are 12 orange flags, how many red ones are there? ....

4 Nathan is one-quarter of his mother's age and three years younger than his sister. If his sister is one-third of their mother's age, how old is Nathan? ....

5 What is the value of half of one-third of one-quarter of £24 000? ....

6 Fill in the missing number:
$\frac{7}{8} \times 16 = \frac{1}{2} \times$ ....

TOP TIP!
Remember: whole numbers can also be written as fractions, e.g. 16 is the same as $\frac{16}{1}$

40 mins

Decimals

7 Fill in the missing number: 10 350.4 × 10 = 207 008 ÷ ....

8 A rectangular room measuring 2.5 m wide and 3.5 m long is fully carpeted. If the carpet costs £12 per square metre, what is the cost of carpeting the room assuming there is no waste?

....

9 A restaurant offers a three-course menu for £17.95 per person. Starters and desserts cost £5.25 each when bought separately, and the main courses vary from £8.50 to £10.50 each.

   a What is the cost for four people to each have a starter and a dessert? ....

   b How much change from £40 do a couple have after both ordering the set menu?

   ....

   c What is the **minimum** amount saved per person if they have the set menu rather than choosing three separate courses? ....

Complete the following equations.

10 1010.305 × 1000 = ...

11 0.0001 × 10^3 = ...

Percentages

12 A farmer has 100 eggs to sell. Two per cent of the eggs break and he packs the rest into boxes of six.

   a How many boxes are filled? ....

   b How many eggs are left over? ....

   c If he gets £2.10 for each dozen, how much money does he make?

   ....

> **TOP TIP!**
>
> **Percent means per 100. Therefore 15% = 15 out of 100, which is the same as $\frac{15}{100}$. It can also be written as a decimal by writing the digits after the decimal point: 15% = 0.15**

13 In a bag of mixed sweets, there are 42 red ones, 17 yellow ones and 22 orange ones. There are 100 sweets altogether. If the rest are green, what **percentage** are green?

....

14 If 30% of an amount of money is £1275, how much is the full amount of money?   £ ....

15 In a school of 500 pupils, 20% learn Latin, 40% learn Spanish and 60% learn French. If half of the pupils learn two languages and no one learns more than two, how many pupils do not learn one of these languages at school?

....

16 A shop sale is offering 10% discount off everything. In the sale, Mrs Down spends £54 on a bag and £81 on a dress. What was the total original cost of these two items before the sale?   ....

NVR Grids

WORKED EXAMPLE

Which pattern completes the larger shape or grid? Underline the answer.

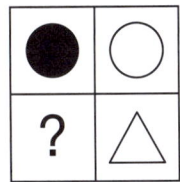 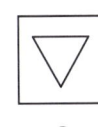 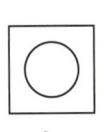   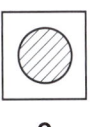

     a   b   c   d   e

The same shape is repeated along each row and the same shading is repeated down each column.

Which pattern completes the larger shape or grid? Underline the answer.

17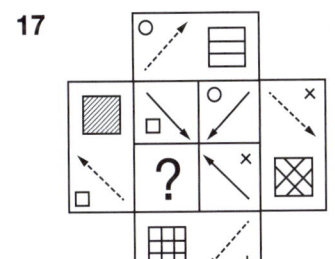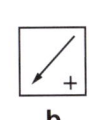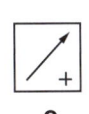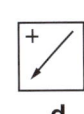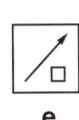

                a   b   c   d   e

18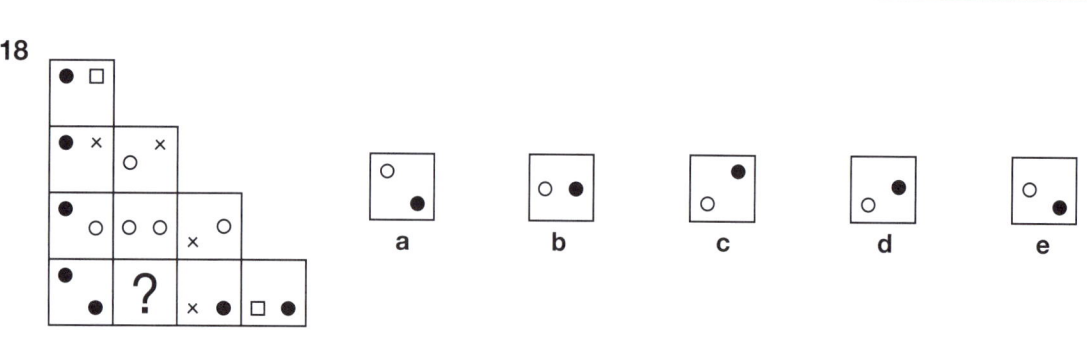

19

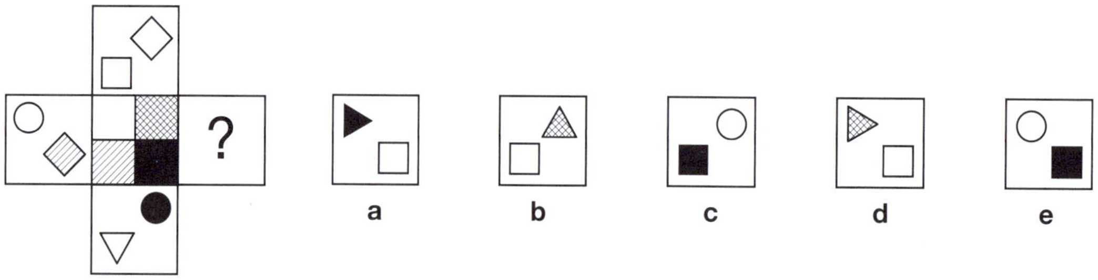

20

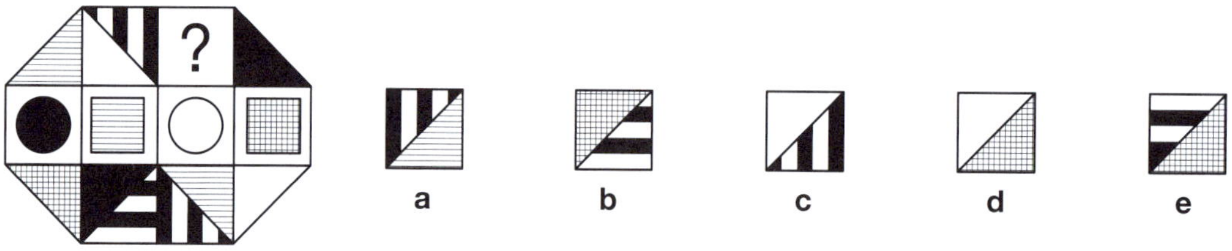

21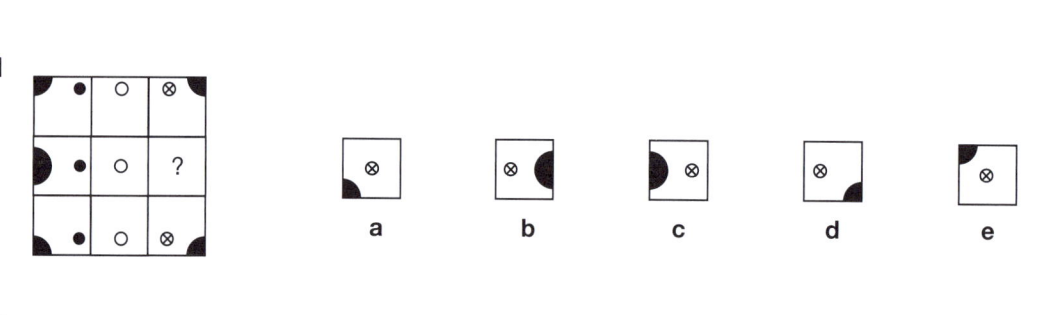

22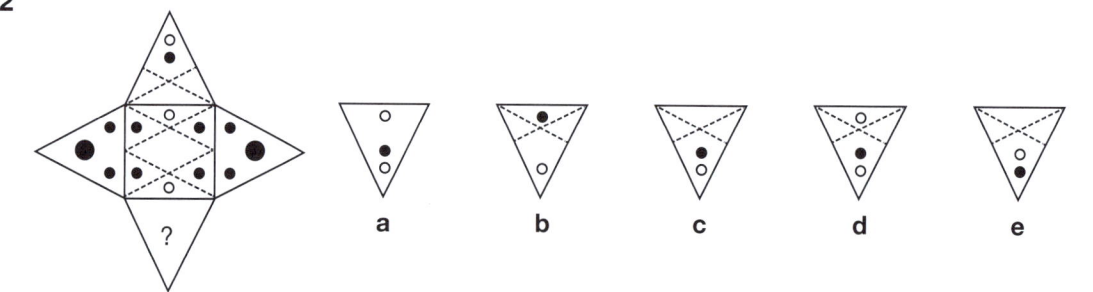

Transformations, Ratios and Proportions

KEY SKILL

A mathematical **ratio** compares two or more numbers which indicate their sizes or amount in relation to each other. For example if two things, A and B, are in the ratio of 1 to 3 then for each one of A, B is three times greater.

Ratios are often written using a colon between the numbers so 1 to 3 is 1:3.

Ratios can compare more than one object, e.g. 1:2:3.

WORKED EXAMPLES

Ratios

Share £36 between 3 children in the ratio of 1:2:3. First find the **total** number of parts needed. 1 + 2 + 3 = 6

Then divide the number or amount given by the number of parts to find the value of each part or portion. 36 ÷ 6 = 6

So one part is 6, two parts are 12 and three parts are 18, and the value of each portion will be £6, £12 and £18.

Reflections

Which pattern on the right is a reflection of the pattern on the left?
Underline the answer.

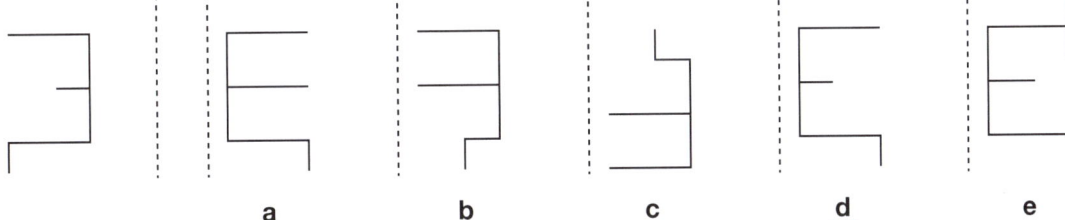

a   b   c   <u>d</u>   e

A reflection is a mirror image of a pattern or shape. Check carefully the elements such as the length of lines, the angles between them, and in some cases the type of shading or number of elements.

In this example in options a, b and c the central horizontal line of the 'E' shape is longer than that in the given pattern. Option e has an extra line added giving a T-shape at the end of one of the horizontal lines, so it is also incorrect. Therefore, the answer is d.

If you find these tricky, practise holding a plain mirror on the dotted line to see the reflection.

Rotations

Which pattern on the right is a rotation of the one on the left? Underline the answer.

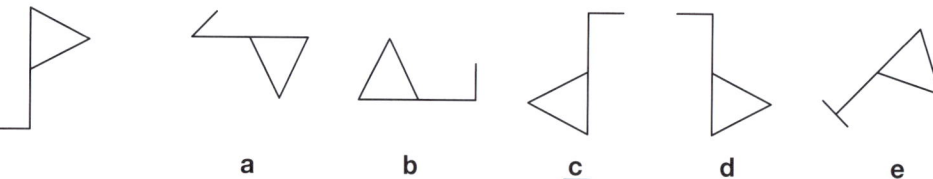

      a   b   <u>c</u>   d   e

When looking for the shape that is a rotation of the shape given, remember the shape itself does not change, just its position on the paper.

Here options a, b and e can be eliminated as the position of the line at the base of the 'flag' shape is different from that given. Option c and d might both look possible at first, but when they are rotated the triangular 'flag' on d will be pointing in the opposite direction, so option c is the answer.

NVR Reflections and Rotations

Which pattern on the right is a reflection of the pattern on the left? Underline the answer.

1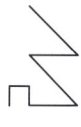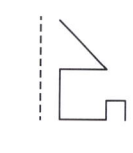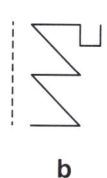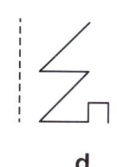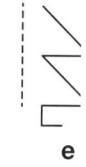

     a   b   c   d   e

2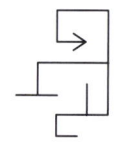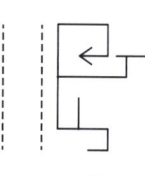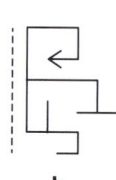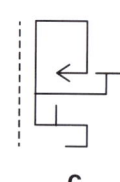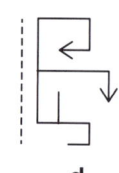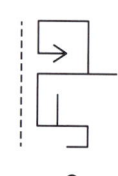

     a   b   c   d   e

3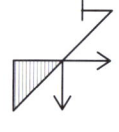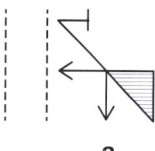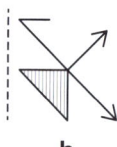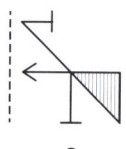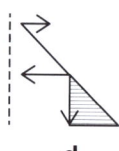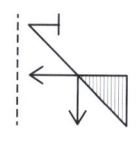

     a   b   c   d   e

4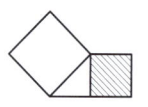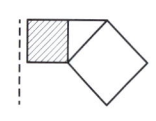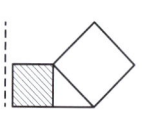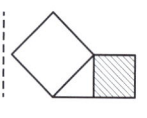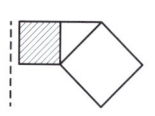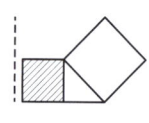

     a   b   c   d   e

5
a b c d e

6
a b c d e

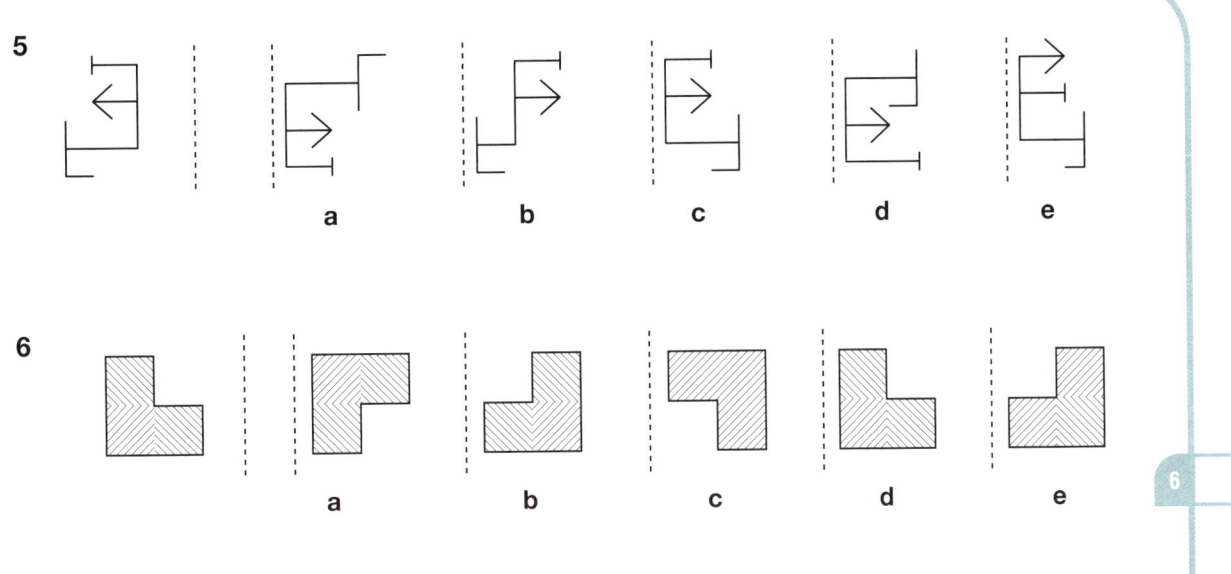

6

Which pattern on the right is a rotation of the one on the left? Underline the answer.

7
a b c d e

8
a b c d e

9
a b c d e

10
a b c d e

4

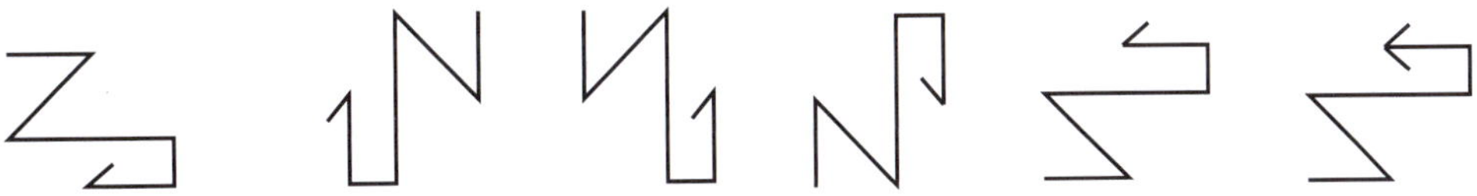

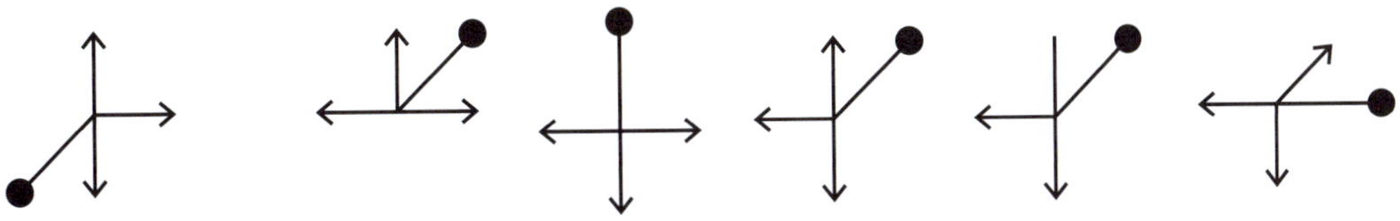

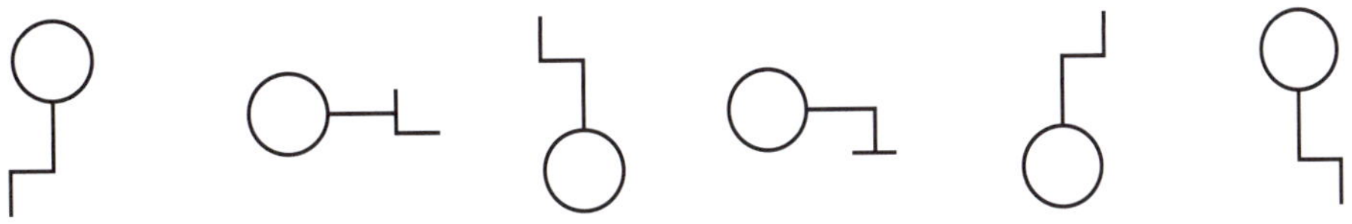

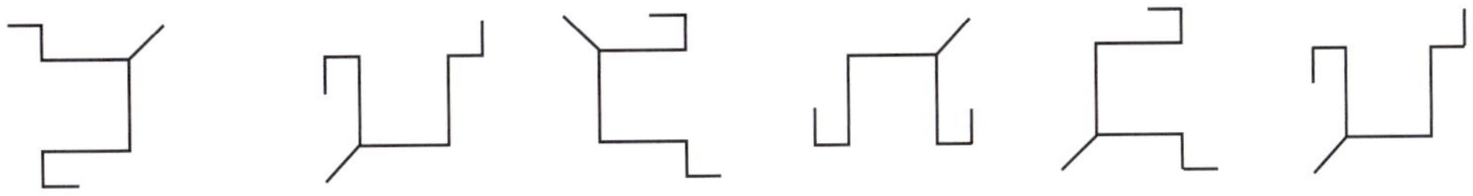

Ratios and Proportions

11 The ingredients for biscuits are sugar, butter and flour in a 1 : 2 : 3 ratio. Using 150 g butter makes 15 biscuits. List the amounts of each ingredient needed to make 45 biscuits.

    a Sugar ....   **b** Butter ....

    c Flour ....

12 A fruit drink is made up of 1 part juice to 2 parts diluted squash. The squash is made up of 1 part concentrate to 4 parts water. How much squash concentrate is needed to make 12 litres of the fruit drink?

....

13 A recipe for 25 cupcakes uses 350 g flour, 250 g butter and 150 g sugar. Complete the list of ingredients to make 35 cupcakes.

    a Flour ....g   **b** Butter ....g

    c Sugar ....g

14 If 15% of an amount of money is £600, how much is the full amount of money?

    £ ....

15 If 1 litre of fuel costs £1.42 and a car does 12 km to the litre, what is the cost of the fuel for a journey of 102 km? ....

16 If 5 apples cost £2.50, what do 12 cost? ....

17 What is a speed of 50 cm per second in metres per minute? ....

18 Flour : butter : sugar are used in the ratio of 7 : 4 : 2 in a recipe. If Beth uses 220 g of sugar, how much flour will be needed? ....

19 If a car uses 1 litre of fuel to go 8 km, and 1 litre costs £1.30, how much will the fuel cost for a journey of 56 km? ....

Total 26

Algebra and Codes

KEY SKILL

Algebra

In algebra, an unknown number is often given a letter.

The multiplication sign is not used in algebra – $4x$ is the same as 4 times x.

An equation is often given to enable you to find the value of the letter.

Remember that when you add, subtract, multiply or divide to solve the equation you must do the same to both sides of the equation in order for them to remain equal.

WORKED EXAMPLE

What is the value of x, if $4x + 7 = 31$?

$$4x + 7 = 31$$
$$-7 \quad -7$$

Subtract 7 from both sides to leave $4x$ on its own:

$$4x = 24$$
$$\div 4 \quad \div 4$$

Then divide both sides by 4 to find the value of one x

$$x = 6$$

BIDMAS

> **TOP TIP!**
>
> **BIDMAS** is a convenient way to remember the order in which calculations are carried out in a sequence of operations. **B**rackets first, then **I**ndices, followed by any **D**ivision and **M**ultiplication, and finally the **A**dditions and **S**ubtractions

1 $(\frac{1}{2} \times \frac{3}{4}) + \frac{1}{2} =$ ....

2 $\frac{3}{5}(120 + 25) =$ ....

3 $(\frac{3}{4} \times 640) + 20 =$ ....

4 $(\frac{30}{4} - \frac{1}{2})(0.3 \times 30) =$ ....

5 $(\frac{1}{2} \times 364) + (\frac{1}{4} \times 48) =$ ....

Algebra

6 If $x = 5$, find the value of: $x^2 + 7x + 3$ ....

7 If $a = 7$, find the value of: $\dfrac{(5a + 3)}{2}$ ....

Find the value of x in the following equations.

8 $3x - 21 = 72$ $x = $ ....

9 $\dfrac{1}{2}x + 14 = 54$ $x = $ ....

10 If $a = 7$, $b = 3$ and $c = 8$, what is the value of the following?

  a $2a + c - b = $ ....   **b** $bc - a + 10 = $ ....   **c** $\dfrac{3c}{b} + 4a = $ ....

11 $10x - 49 = 3x$, $x = $ ....

If $a = 5$, $b = 11$ and $c = 4$, what is the value of the following?

12 $2b + 2a^2 - \dfrac{c}{2} = $ ....

13 $\dfrac{(3a + 3b)}{c} = $ ....

What is the value of x if:

14 $3x + 12 = 5x$ $x = $ ....

15 $21x - 4 = 5x + 60$ $x = $ ....

NVR Codes

WORKED EXAMPLE

Which code matches the shape or pattern given at the end of each line?
Underline the answer.

AX   BY   CX   BZ   ?

AY CZ BX CY AZ
a   b   <u>c</u>   d   e

When letter codes are given to shapes, the first letter in the code will always refer to the same element of the shapes, so look carefully to see what the shapes with the same letter have in common. Here the two shapes with B are wide ovals, and A and C are different shapes. So A is a circle, B is a wide oval and C a 'tall' oval. The answer code will start with B.

The second letter will apply to a different element. Again look carefully at the shapes that share a letter. There are two with an X, what do they have in common? Here the two shapes with X have diagonal lines, so the second letter refers to shading style. X has diagonal lines, Y has small squares and Z has horizontal lines. So the answer code will have X, giving BX.

In questions with three-letter codes there will be a further third element to identify.

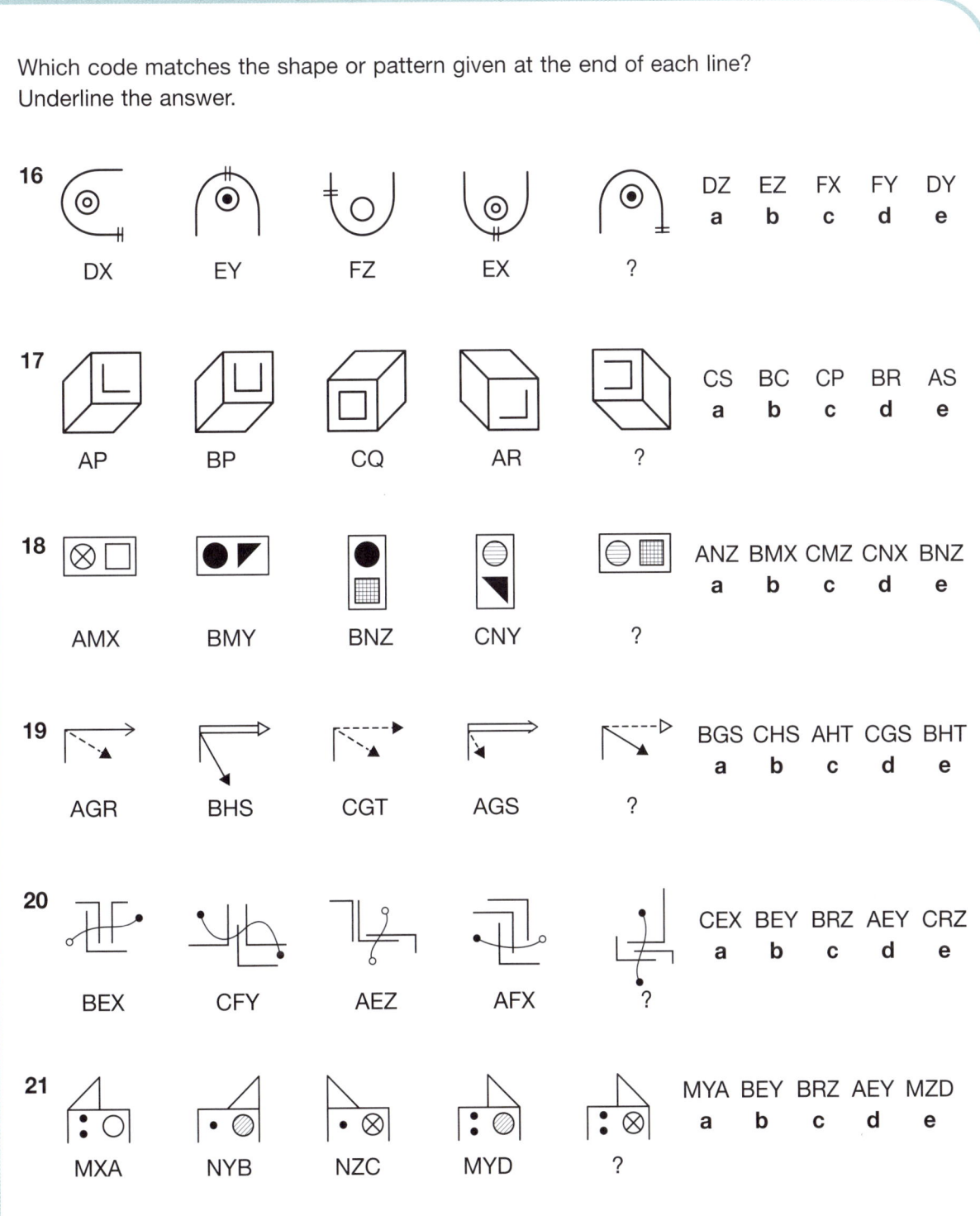

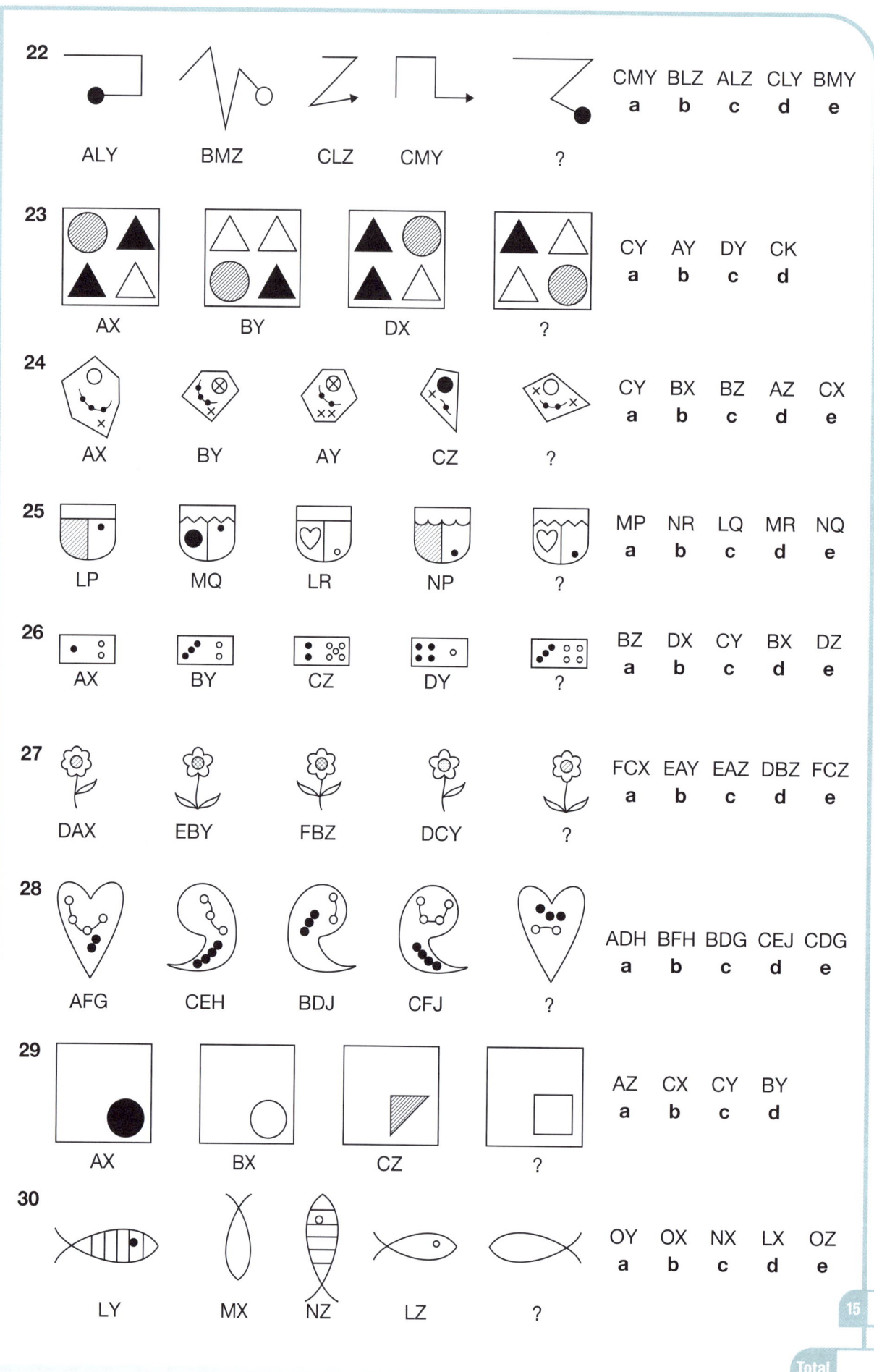

Measurement

KEY SKILL

To answer questions involving measurements there are some key facts that must be known:

1000 mm = 100 cm = 1 m, 1000 m = 1 km

1000 mg = 1 g, 1000 g = 1 kg

1000 ml = 1 litre

60 seconds = 1 minute, 60 minutes = 1 hour, 24 hours = 1 day

The **perimeter** of a shape is the distance around the edge, it is found by adding together the lengths of all of the sides of the shape.

The **area** of a shape is the amount of surface, it is measured in square units. This can be written in two ways, e.g. for an area calculated from measurements in cm, area can be written as 'square cm' or 'cm^2'.

Volume is a measure of the space occupied by a solid or 3D shape, it is measured in cubic units. This can be written in two ways, e.g. for a volume calculated from measurements in cm, volume can be written as 'cubic cm' or 'cm^3'.

WORKED EXAMPLE

What is the total surface area of a **cube** that has sides 5 cm long? What is its **volume**?

Each face of the cube is a square, 5 cm × 5 cm, so the area of each face is $25\,cm^2$.

A cube has 6 faces all the same size, so the total surface area is $25\,cm^2 \times 6 = 150\,cm^2$

The volume of a cube is the length × width × height = 5 cm × 5 cm × 5 cm = **$125\,cm^3$**

Conversions

1 0.5 kg + 120 g + 400 mg = ... g

2 Convert 0.3 km to mm ....

3 How many cm are there in 1.5 km? ....

4 How many mm are there in 0.75 km? ....

5 How many ml are left if 760 ml are taken from 4.2 litres? .... ml

TOP TIP!

When converting metric units remember to check the number of zeros and/or the position of the decimal point very carefully

6 How many metres are in 170 m plus 300 cm plus 0.26 km? .... m

7 What is the **difference** in kg between 6.35 kg and 10 050 g? .... kg

8 What is the total length in cm of 46 mm, 3.2 cm and 0.42 m? .... cm

9 How many mm are there in 3.4 km? .... mm

Perimeter, Area and Volume

10 A warehouse charges £35 per week to store 4 cubic metres of goods. How much will it cost a company to store a container measuring 20 m × 5 m × 3 m for 2 weeks?

....

11 A 2½ litre can of emulsion covers 24 square metres of wall surface. The walls in a square room are 6 metres long and 2 metres high. How many litres of emulsion are needed to give all four walls two coats of paint?

....

12 What is the **perimeter** of a regular **heptagon** with sides of 3.5 cm? ....

13 If 1 ml of water occupies 1 cubic centimetre how many litres of water can a 10 cm cube hold?

....

14 The four sides of a field measure 430 m, 310 m, 360 m and 400 m respectively. How many times must a jogger go round the field to complete a 12 km run?

....

15 The perimeter of a rectangle 3 cm wide is 32 cm. What is its length? ....

16 A cube with sides of 6 cm is built out of 1 cm cubes. The outside of the large cube is painted red. How many of the smaller 1 cm cubes will have:

a 2 faces painted red? ....   **b** 3 faces painted red? ....

c no red faces? ....

Time

17 Some friends set off at 9.00 a.m. on a 16 km walk. If they **average** 4 km per hour, at what time will they be halfway?

> **TOP TIP!**
> When doing calculations with time, remember there are 60 minutes in an hour

....

18 How long does it take a driver travelling at 60 km per hour to drive the 48 km from Alston to Castleford if he includes a 25-minute break halfway?

....

19 A farmer's herd of dairy cattle give 200 gallons of milk every morning.

  a If the cows are milked twice each day and each cow on average gives 4 gallons a day, how many cows are in the herd?

  ....

  b If Daisy, the cow producing the most milk, actually gives 50% more than the average, how much milk does Daisy give in a full week?

  ....

20 A train leaves Bidden at 14:37 and arrives at the next station, Carbury, at 15:07. The train travels at an average speed of 80 km per hour. The same journey by road is 10 km longer.

  a How far is it from Bidden to Carbury by train? ....

  b How long will it take a car travelling at 50 m per hour to get from Bidden to Carbury?   ....

21 If a car travels at 60 km per hour for the first half of a 120 km journey, and covers the second half of the journey in half the time of the first half, how long does the total journey take?

....

22 High tide is at 03:12 hours one day.

  a If the tide took 6 hours and 17 minutes to come in, at what time was the previous low tide? ....

  b If it takes the same amount of time to go out, when will the next low tide be?

  ....

Total 34

Geometry and Nets

KEY SKILL

Check that you know the properties of these 2D shapes. You can refer to the definitions of these in the Keywords on page 92.

- triangles have 3 sides – **equilateral**, right angled, isosceles, scalene
- **quadrilaterals** have 4 sides – square, rectangle, **parallelogram**, **rhombus**, trapezium, **kite**
- a **hexagon** has 6 sides, a **heptagon** has 7 sides, an octagon has 8 sides and a decagon has 10 sides.

Check that you know the properties of these 3D shapes and can recognise the nets that can form them:

- cube, **cuboid**, cylinder, **prism** and pyramid.

Learn these four basic angle rules:

- angles around a point add up to 360°
- angles on a straight line add up to 180°
- angles in a triangle add up to 180°
- angles in a quadrilateral add up to 360°.

Angles are measured in **degrees**. A complete rotation is 360 degrees. Direction of rotation can be described as clockwise or anticlockwise.

The hands on a clockface and the points of a compass can be used to describe angle or rotation.

- Between each number on a clockface there is an angle of 30°
- Between the compass points of N-NE, NE-E, E-SE, etc. is an angle of 45°.

WORKED EXAMPLES

Through how many degrees does the big hand of a clock rotate between 8 o'clock and 8.35 a.m.?

There are 30° between each number on the clockface, that is 30° for every 5 minutes.

So in 35 minutes the big hand has rotated through 30° × 7 = **210°**

How many edges are there on a hexagonal prism?

There is a hexagon at the each end of the prism – so that is 6 × 2 edges = 12 edges

There are 6 edges joining each corner of the hexagon at one end with the hexagon at the other end of the prism.

So a hexagonal prism has 12 + 6 = **18 edges**

Angles

1 Find the value of the third angle in these triangles:

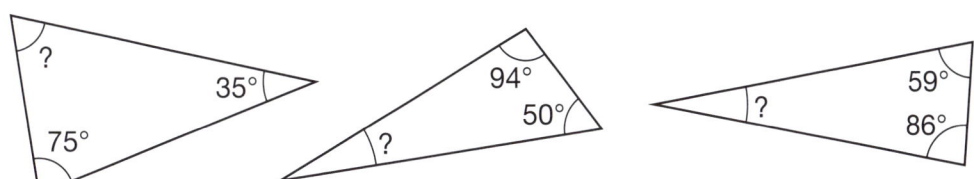

a .... b .... c ....

Look carefully at the following diagrams to calculate these angles and explain your answers.

2

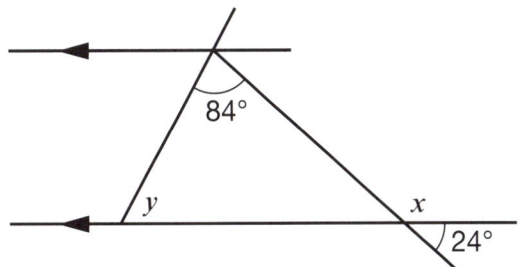

a Angle x = ...

Because ....

b Angle y = ...

Because ....

3

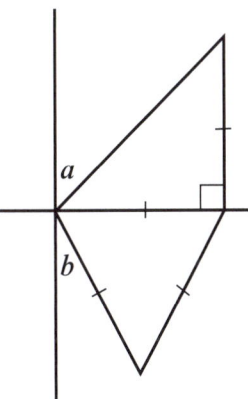

a Angle a = ...

Because ....

b Angle b = ...

Because ....

Position and Direction

4 Sam is facing north. First he turns 135° clockwise. Then he turns 180° clockwise.

   a In which direction is he now facing? ....

   b Describe the direction and angle of the turn he must make to move from that position to a position where he is facing East.

   ....

5 This graph shows three points making a triangle.

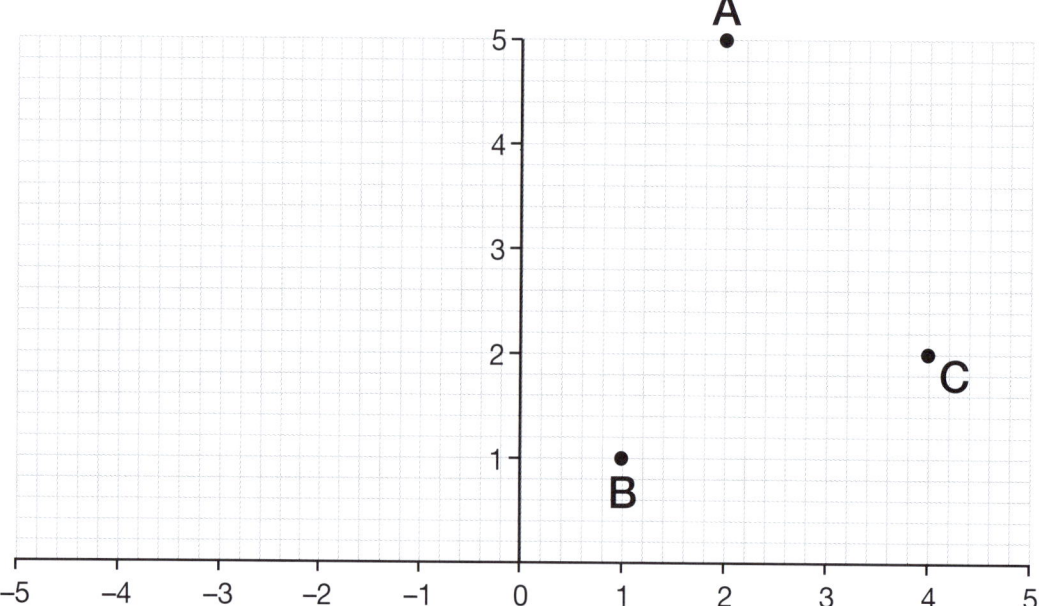

If triangle A, B, C is reflected in the y axis, what are the new **coordinates** for its three corners, A', B' and C'?

A' ....

B' ....

C' ....

> **coordinate** A pair of numbers used to locate a point. The first number is the distance along the horizontal line and the second number is the distance along the vertical line

6 Look at the points on the graph below and then answer the questions.

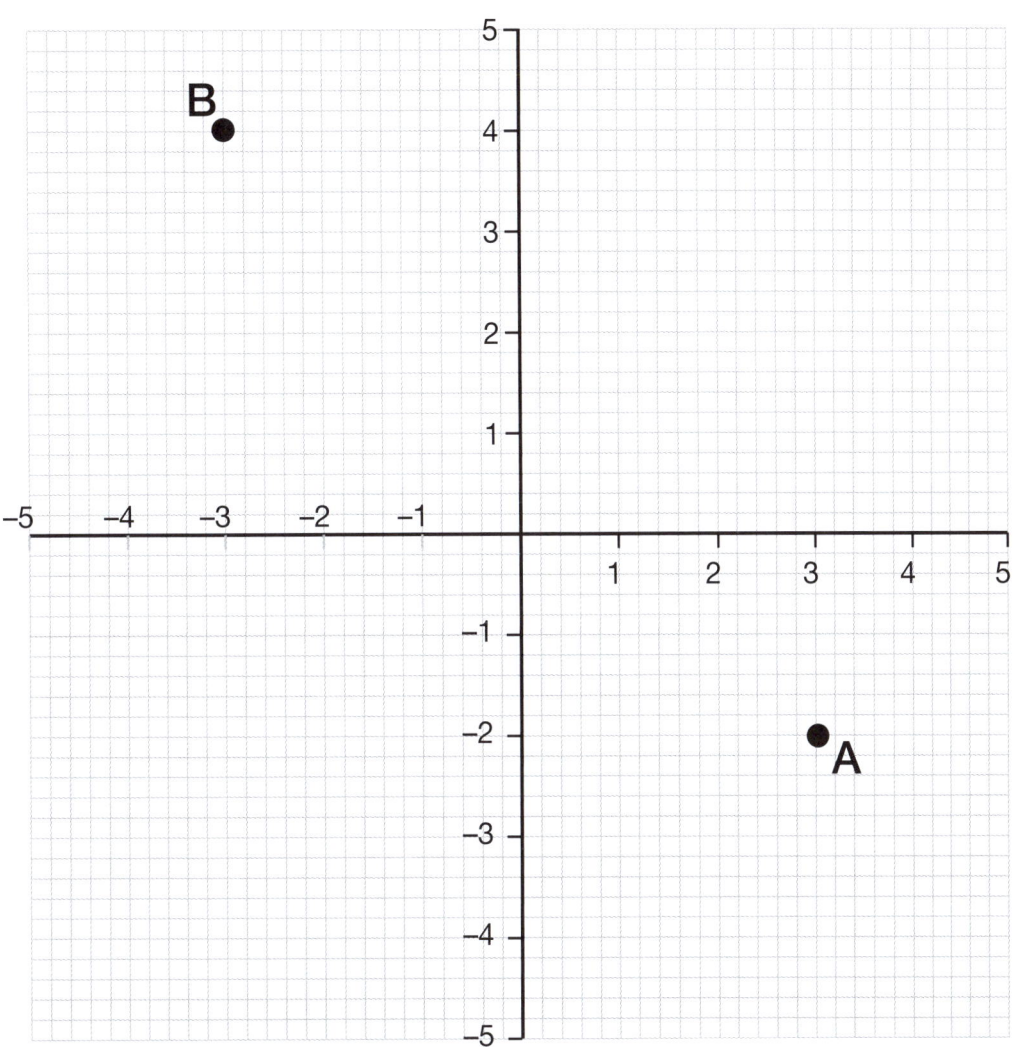

a What are the coordinates for point A on the graph?

....

b If point B is reflected in the *y* axis, what will its coordinates be in the reflected image?

....

c If point B is reflected in the *x* axis, what are the coordinates for the point in the image?

....

NVR Nets

WORKED EXAMPLE

Which cube cannot be made from the net on the left? Underline the answer.

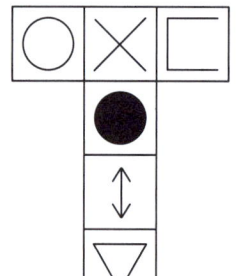 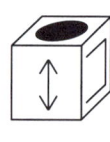 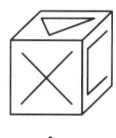 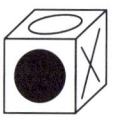 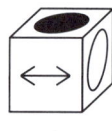 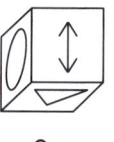

                                          a   b   c   <u>d</u>   e

If the squares of these nets are numbered, then squares 1 and 3, 2 and 5, and 4 and 6 will end up as opposite faces in the cube, so those patterns cannot be adjacent.

Three squares in a row in the net – 1, 2, 3 or 2, 4, 5 or 4, 5, 6 or 5, 6, 2 – will not all be seen in the cube at the same time.

The patterns on squares 1 and 3 can be adjacent to any of the other squares (except each other), but their orientation will change as the net is folded. So, in the worked example, the arrow will not point towards the white circle or the U-shape but can be adjacent to them. So it is cube d that cannot be made as the arrow points to the face with the white circle.

TOP TIP!

Read the question carefully. Sometimes it asks for the cube that *cannot* be made and sometimes for the one that *can* be made

Which cube cannot be made from the net on the left? Underline the answer.

7

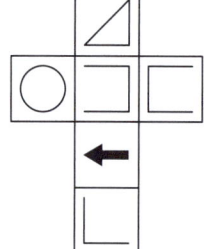 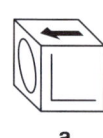    

                                          a   b   c   d   e

8

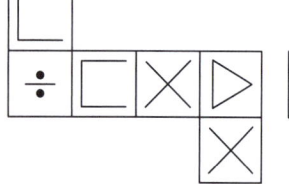  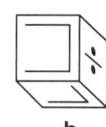   

                                          a   b   c   d   e

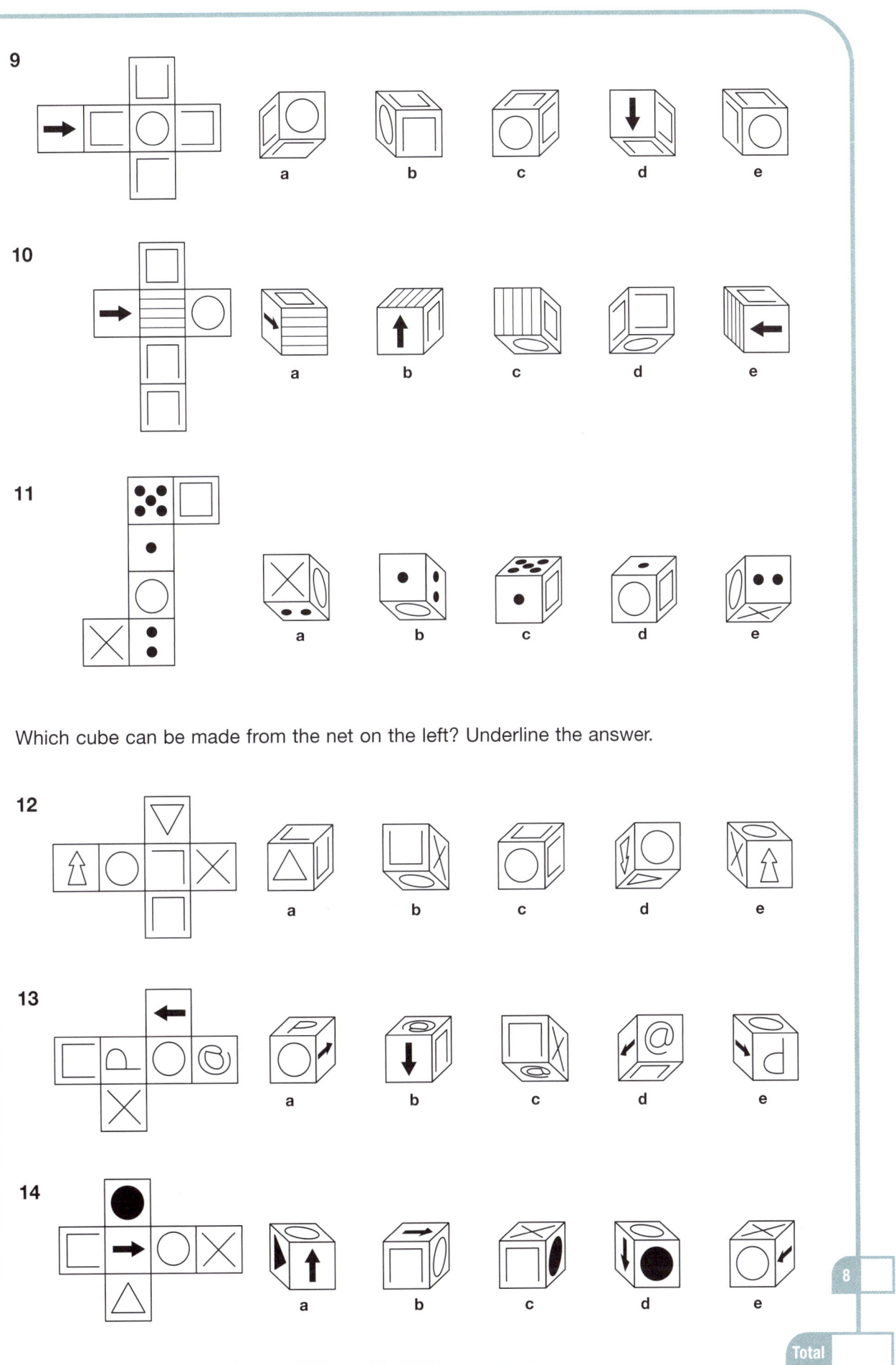

Which cube can be made from the net on the left? Underline the answer.

Statistics

> ### KEY SKILL
>
> Data can be presented in different ways, including tables, charts and graphs.
>
> - When reading data from tables follow the rows and columns carefully
> - When plotting, or reading data from, graphs check the scale used – it might not be the same on both axes
> - **Pie charts** use a whole circle to represent all of the data, with sectors drawn according to the proportion of the whole that they represent
> - Pictograms use symbols to represent data and they have a key to show the value of each symbol.
>
> To find the **average** of two or more numbers, you add the values together and divide by the number of values.
>
> The **mean** value of a set of data is the same as the average.
>
> The **range** is a measure of the spread of the values, it is calculated by subtracting the lowest value from the highest value.

WORKED EXAMPLE

Child	A	B	C	D	E	F	G	H	I	J
1st	18	15	10	14	8	20	12	18	15	20
2nd	20	18	16	18	15	20	18	19	16	20

This table records the marks out of 20 gained by 10 pupils in 2 tests.

What is the **difference** between the average score of the first test and the average score of the second test?

Add together the scores for each test and divide by 10, the number of test scores in the set:

The average score for the 1st test is 18 + 15 + 10 + 14 + 8 + 20 + 12 + 18 + 15 + 20 = 150
150 ÷ 10 = **15**

The average score for the 2nd test is 20 + 18 + 16 + 18 + 15 + 20 + 18 + 19 + 16 + 20 = 180
180 ÷ 10 = **18**

Subtract the averages to find the difference: 18 − 15 = **3**

What is the **range** of marks in the first test?

Highest − lowest is 20 − 8 = **12**

Bar Charts

1 Children in a class were asked to name their favourite fruit. The results were recorded in this bar chart:

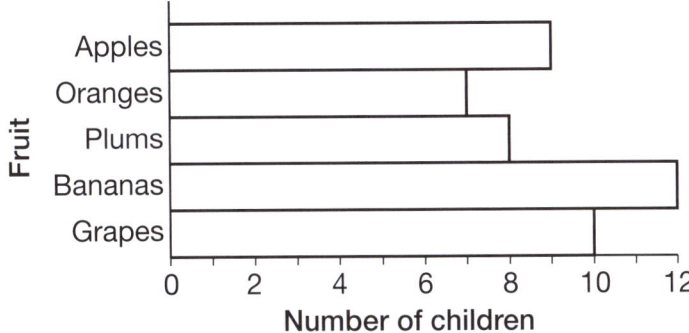

a How many children were asked? ....

b Which fruits were chosen by more than 20% of the class? ....

c If one-third of the children who chose bananas changed their choice to apples, how many more children will have chosen apples than oranges?

....

2 The graph shows the test scores for ten pupils given as a percentage.

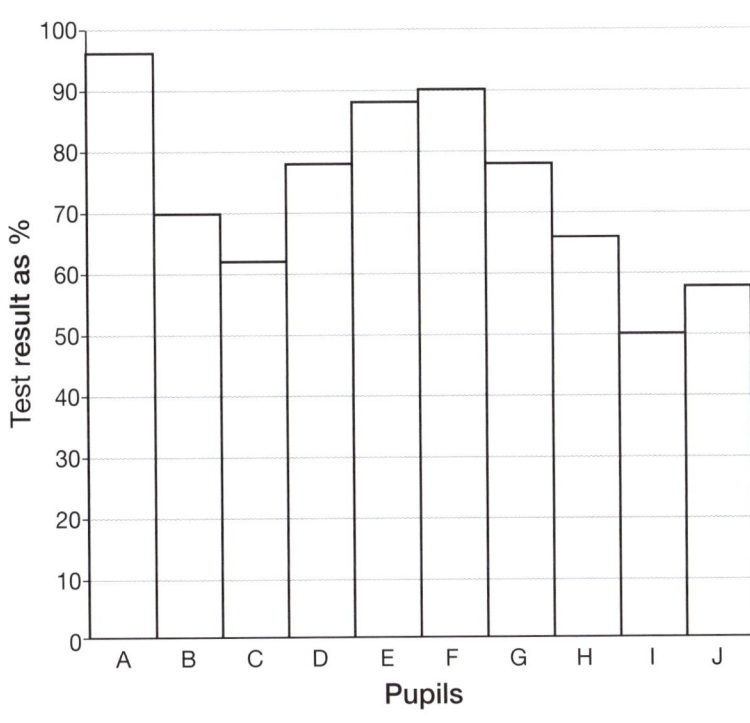

TOP TIP!

If the scale on an axis does not mark each separate division, you need to make a careful estimate of the value when reading off the graph

a What same percentage score was achieved by two pupils? ....

b If there were 50 marks in the test, how many
   marks were gained by the pupil with the highest score?   ....

c Which pupil gained 31 marks? ....

d What was the average percentage score for the three pupils H, I and J?

....

Line Graphs

3   This chart shows the details of Toby's journey to a friend's house.

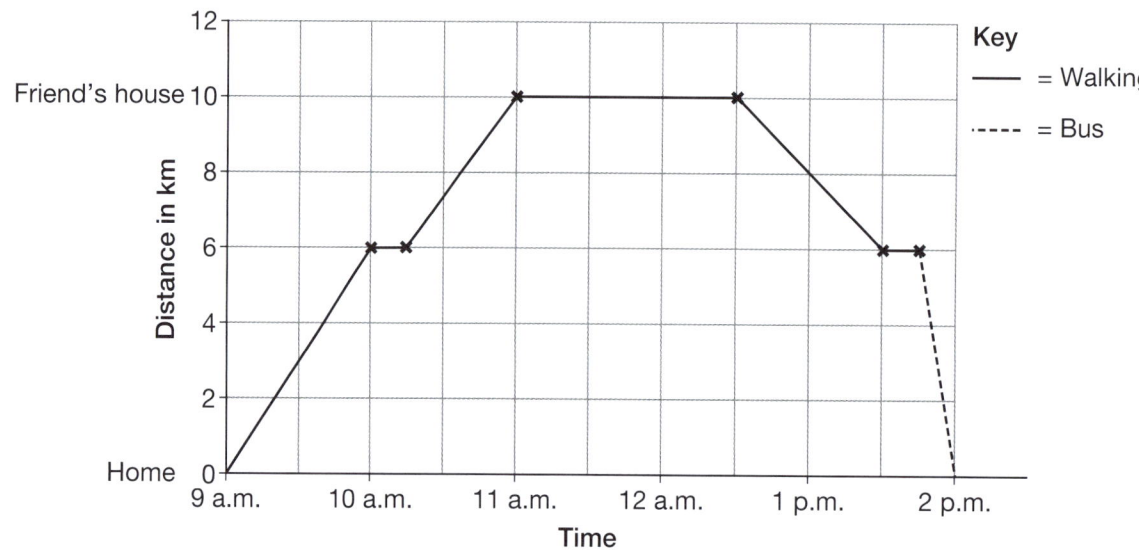

a Toby walks to a friend's house 10 km away, taking a
   short rest along the way. How long was he walking for?   ....

b On the return journey, he walks part of the way and
   then gets the bus. At what time did he get on the bus?   ....

c How long was Toby at his friend's house?   ....

d How many kilometres did Toby walk in total?   ....

4 This graph shows the height of a seedling each day after germination.

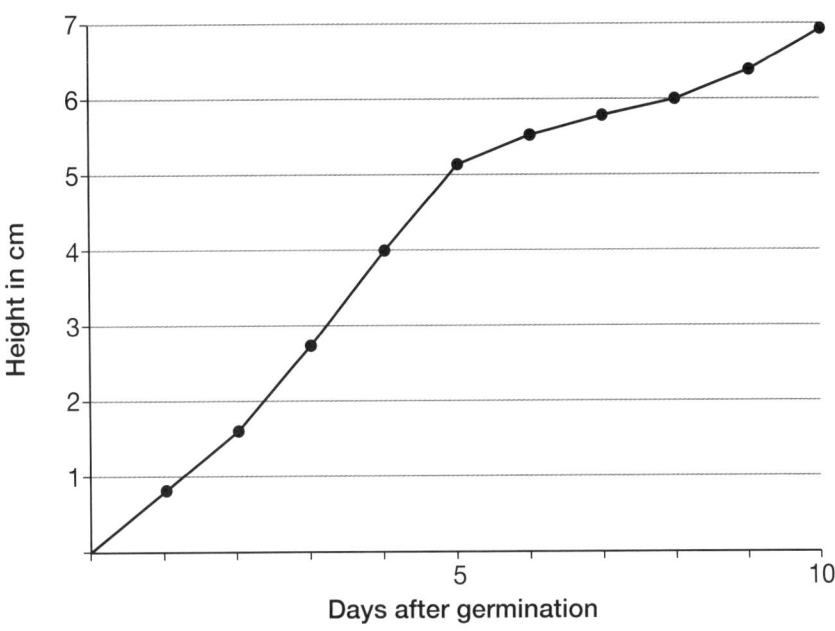

    a After how many days was the seedling 6 cm high? ....

    b What was its average rate of growth over the first ten days? ....

    c If the rate of growth is slowest on the coldest day,
   which of the ten days was the coldest? ....

    d Which four consecutive days have an average rate
   of growth of 1 cm per day? ....

Tables

5 Ten children are growing sunflowers.

	Height of sunflower in cm
Annie	168
Soma	203
Taya	154
Lea	101
Max	94
Nat	180
Carl	213
Ella	142
Toby	161
Felix	207

a What is the range of the heights? ....

b By how much more will Annie's sunflower need to grow to be the same height as Felix's? ....

6 This chart shows the distances in kilometres between five villages.

	Radford	Sandon	Towie	Umber	Vacton
Radford		34	27	53	28
Sandon	34		40	45	36
Towie	27	40		48	70
Umber	53	45	48		24
Vacton	28	36	70	24	

a How far is it from Radford to Vacton? ....

b How much closer is Sandon to Towie than it is to Umber? ....

c If a car travels at 60 km per hour, how long will it take to get from Towie to Vacton?

....

7 In a game of Paldi, the highest possible score is 20 points. Three friends played six rounds of the game and recorded their point scores in the table below.

	Round 1	Round 2	Round 3	Round 4	Round 5	Round 6	TOTAL
Ginny	12	15	14	16	15	18	
Harry	10	12	13	17	18	20	
Indigo	14	16	16	17	13	19	

a Complete the 'Total' column. ....

b What was Ginny's average point score per round? ....

c Who had the widest range in the point scores? ....

d What was the total number of points in the highest-scoring round? ....

8 The table shows the number of points gained by each team in a series of five games.

The three teams with the highest number of points qualify for the next round.

	Game 1	Game 2	Game 3	Game 4	Game 5
Team A	3	4	0	2	4
Team B	3	5	4	2	3
Team C	0	3	1	2	4
Team D	2	3	2	1	3
Team E	4	5	2	3	1

a Which two teams will not qualify? ....

b What was Team E's mean (average) point score? ....

c What was Team B's final point score? ....

9 This table records the goal scores for matches between five different teams. The score of the team named on the left is shown first.

Teams	A	B	C	D	E
A		2–4	1–3	5–4	2–3
B	4–2		1–0	4–3	5–3
C	3–1	0–1		3–1	2–2
D	4–5	3–4	1–3		1–3
E	3–2	3–5	2–2	3–1	

a How many goals did Team A score in total? ....

b How many matches were played? ....

c How many matches did Team D win? ....

d What was Team C's goal average? ....

e Which team won all of its matches? ....

f If there are 2 points for a win, 1 for a draw and none for a loss, complete this table giving point scores:

	Points
Team A	
Team B	
Team C	
Team D	
Team E	

Averages

10 A lorry driver averages 540 km distance per day, with an average **speed** of 60 km per hour. How many hours will he be driving for during a five-day working week?

....

11 This chart shows a town's average monthly rainfall in mm.

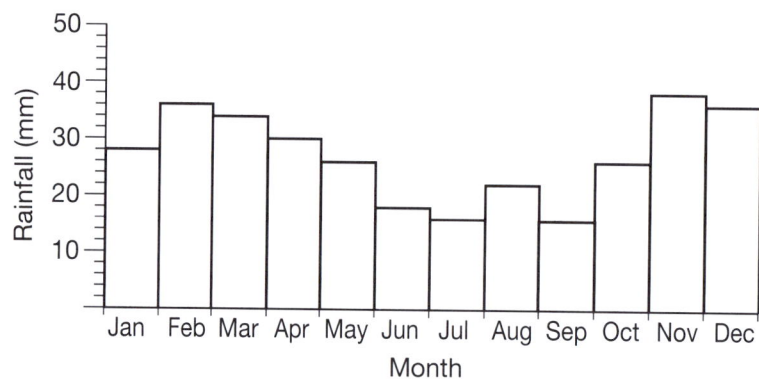

a How many months have a mean rainfall greater than 35 mm? ....

b What is the average rainfall from the start of June to the end of September?

....

c What is the range of average monthly rainfall measurements across the year in mm?   ....

12 A cyclist travels at 20 km per hour and a car averages 50 km per hour. Oliver and Pete agree to meet at 11.00 a.m. at a castle 30 km away. If Oliver cycles and Pete takes the car, how much earlier must Oliver leave the house than Pete?

....

Pie Charts

13 Here is a **pie chart** showing the favourite lunch choices of a group of students.

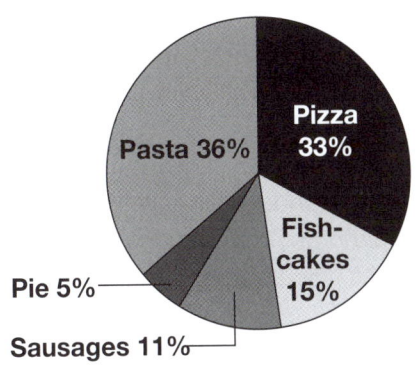

a If this chart showed the results for a class of 20 children, how many chose pie?

....

b If the data was collected in a school of 500 pupils, how many chose fishcakes?

....

c Which two choices could be offered that would please at least half of the children?

....

d One-third of the children chose pizza. What is the size of the angle on the pie chart for the section representing pizza?

....

e Connie wanted to make a pie chart for her own family, with three choosing pizza, one curry and two spaghetti. What size angle must she draw in the circle for the curry sector?

....

Curveball Questions 1

1. Mr Rafiz has a large rectangular pond 2.5 m wide and 8 m long. Water evaporates from the surface of his pond at the rate of 50 ml per square metre per hour when the sun is out.

   He has a hosepipe to top up the pond. If it is turned on to give a slow steady flow of 7 litres per hour, for how many hours must he have the hosepipe turned on to refill the pond after one week of sunny days, assuming the sun was out for eight hours each day?

2. Complete this pattern so that there is a vertical line of symmetry down the middle and a horizontal line of symmetry across the middle.

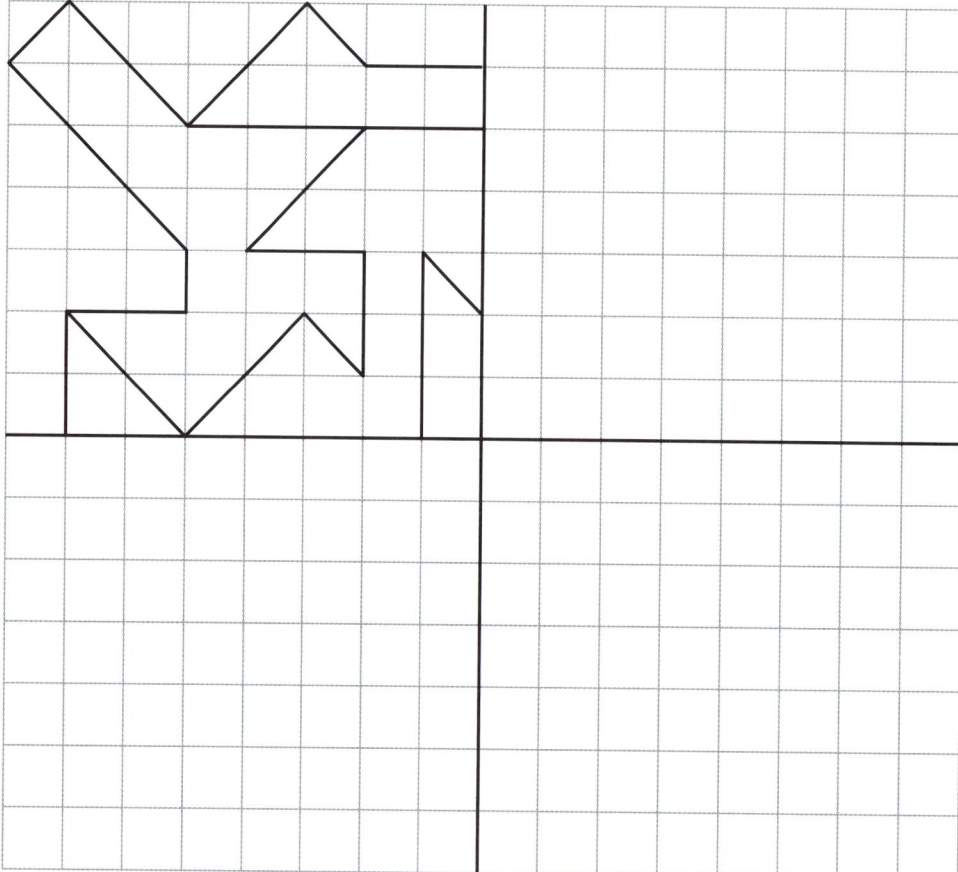

3 Complete this number crossword using the number clues below.

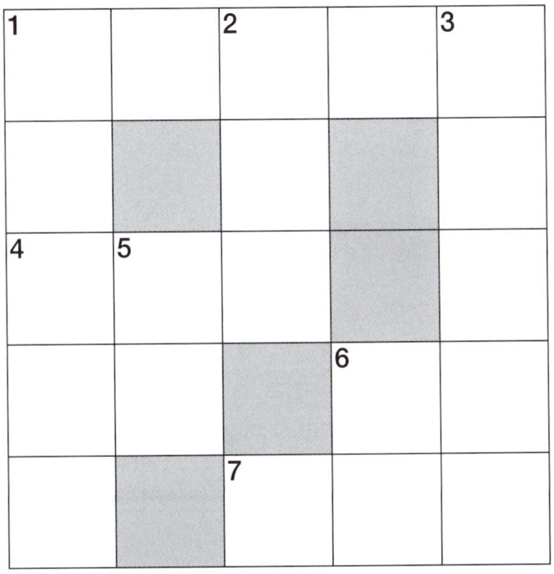

Across

1 15 022 + 6204

4 1000 − 1

6 7^2

7 10 dozen

Down

1 (100 000 ÷ 4) − 70

2 73 × 3

3 32 210 less than 100 000

5 31 × 3

6 6 × 7

9

Total 15

Mixed Papers

Mixed Paper 1

NVR Analogies

Which pattern completes the second pair in the same way as the first pair? Underline the answer.

WORKED EXAMPLE

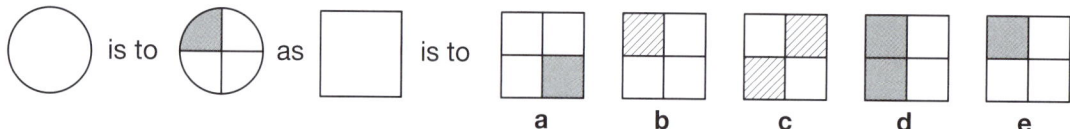

The second shape is the same as the first shape but divided into quarters, with the top left quarter shaded grey. In the answer options given here they are all squares divided into quarters, so it is necessary to look for the one that has the top left quarter shaded grey.

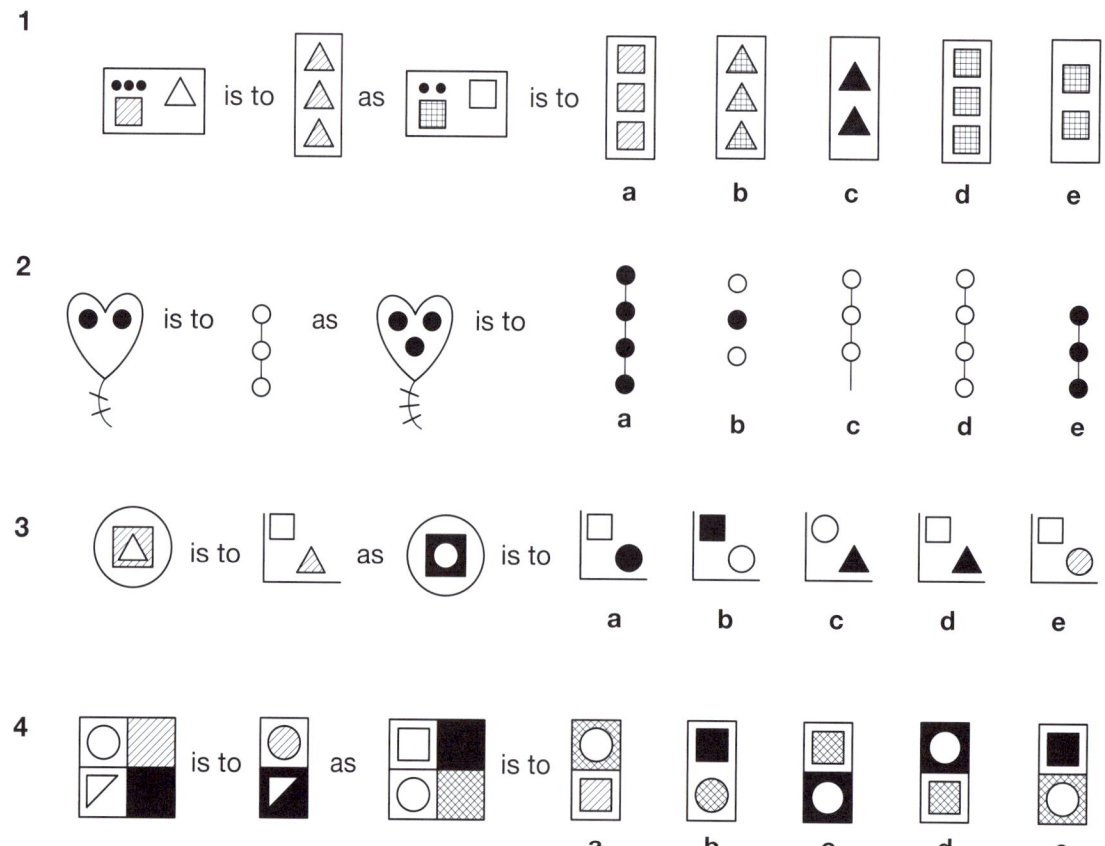

Place value

5 What is the **total** of the digits in the hundreds column and in the hundredths column of these three numbers?

5473.0516   108.023   1298.619   ....

6 Write the number seventeen million, seventy two thousand, seven hundred and two in digits.

....

7 What is five hundred and three point four less than one thousand? Write the answer in words.

....

8 What is 110 000 less than 22 million? ....

Word and Logic Problems

9 Pete had five packages, labelled A, B, C, D and E.
Package A weighed 3.0 kg.
Package C was 250 g heavier than D and 500 g lighter than E.
Package B was 500 g heavier than D and 500 g lighter than A.

   a How much did package B weigh? ....

   b Which was the heaviest package? ....

   c Which was the lightest package? ....

10 A shop sells twice as many vanilla as strawberry flavour ice creams, and twice as many chocolate as vanilla. If it sells 60 strawberry ice creams, what was the total number of ice creams sold?

....

11 Tim spends £1.75 on chocolates, 80p on a paper and £1.15 on a drink, and he pays with a £5 note. When he gets home, he finds he has only two of the three coins given in change. If he has a pound coin and a 20p coin, what was the value of the coin he lost?

....

Percentages

12 Goods imported valued at £400 are subject to a 15% tax.

  a How much tax will have to be paid? ....

  b How much will the importer need to sell the goods for to cover the cost of the tax and to give a 10% profit on the value of the goods?

  ....

13 Tim inherits £1000 from his aunt. If she has left 20% of her money to charity and given Tim 5% of her money, how much has she given to charity?

....

14 If a monthly rent of £520 is increased by 3%, what is the new monthly rent?

....

NVR Grids

Which shape or pattern on the right completes the grid on the left? Underline the answer.

15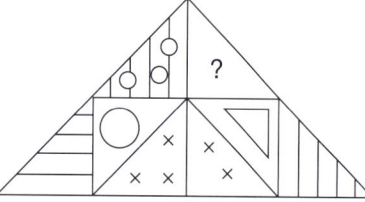
                                                                                                a   **b**   **c**   **d**   **e**

16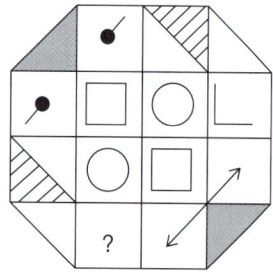

17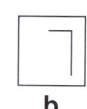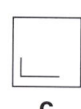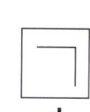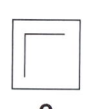
       a   **b**   **c**   **d**   **e**

18

a 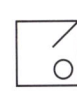 b  c 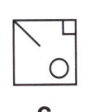 d  e

Algebra

19 What is the value of x if $52x + 10 = 166$? $x = $ ....

20 $6x + 5 = 3y - 10$

   a If $y = 11$, what is the value of x?   ....

   b If $x = 5$, what is the value of y?   ....

21 If $a = 4$ and $b = 10$, what is the value of:

   a $3ab = $ ....

   b $\frac{4b}{8} + 7 = $ ....

   c $a^2 + b^2 + 42 = $ ....

NVR Codes

Which code matches the shape on the right? Underline the answer.

22

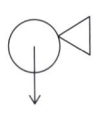  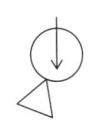 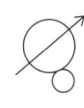 

AX   BY   CX   BZ   ?

AZ	BX	CY	CZ	AY
a	b	c	d	e

23

 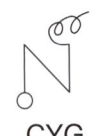 

AXF   BXE   CYG   DZF   ?

AZE	BYG	DXF	BYF	DYE
a	b	c	d	e

24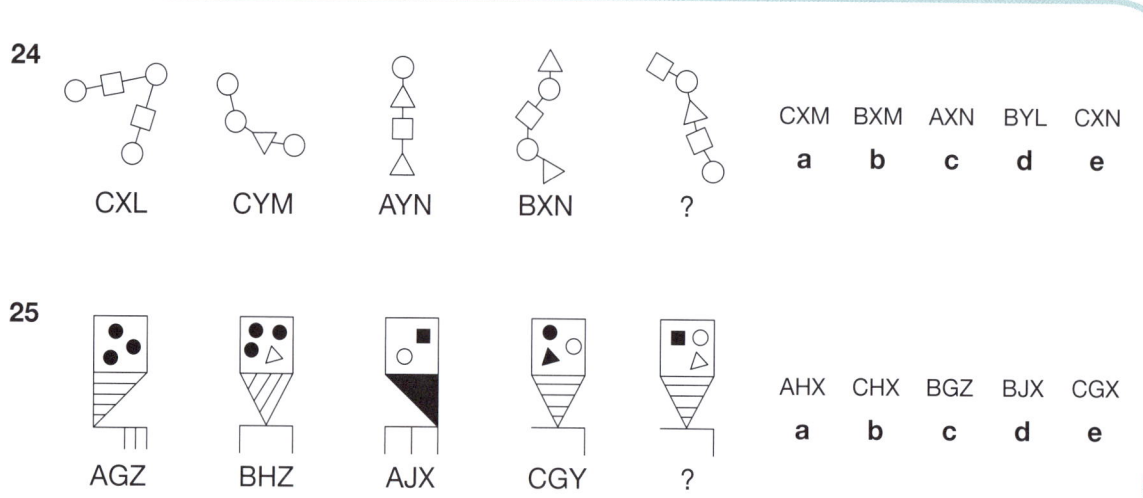

	CXM	BXM	AXN	BYL	CXN
	a	b	c	d	e

CXL   CYM   AYN   BXN   ?

25

	AHX	CHX	BGZ	BJX	CGX
	a	b	c	d	e

AGZ   BHZ   AJX   CGY   ?

Position and Direction

Use this information to answer the next two questions.

The route taken by a sailing boat was tracked every hour. It started travelling north. After one hour it turned 45° anticlockwise, and then made a 90° turn clockwise after 30 minutes. It continued sailing in that direction for two hours. It then turned 45° clockwise and sailed for another 20 minutes to its destination.

26 In what direction was the boat sailing for the last 20 minutes? ....

27 If the boat left at 9.30 a.m., what time did it arrive at its destination?

....

28 Jack has a remote control car which responds to directions to turn that are given in angles, with the instruction 'right' for clockwise and 'left' for anticlockwise, otherwise it travels in a straight line. The car is facing south and Jack gives it these instructions when it sets off: R 30°, L 120°, L 45°, L 90°, R 180°. What direction was the car travelling in after following these instructions?

....

29 A drone is set to draw a smoke pattern in the sky. It turns from north to north-east, to east, to south-east, to south, to south-west, to west, to north-west and back to north. What shape has it drawn in the sky?

....

Bar Charts

30 This graph shows the favourite sports of a group of students.

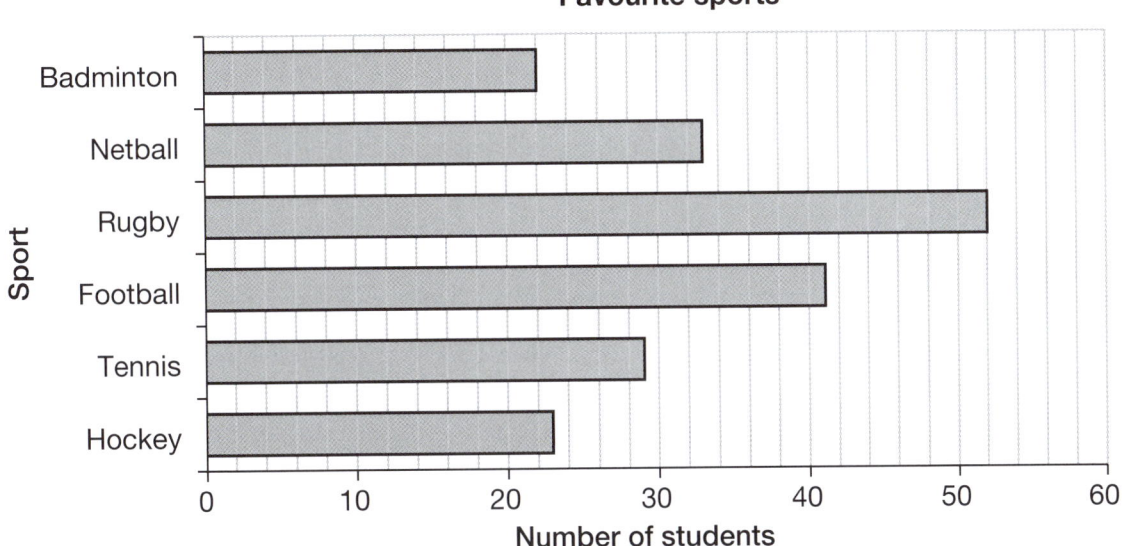

  a How many students chose rugby as their favourite sport? ....

  b How many more chose netball than badminton? ....

  c How many students were asked altogether? ....

  d What is the smallest number of extra players needed to make up complete netball teams with seven in each team allowing all those who chose netball to play?

  ....

Mixed Paper 2

NVR Analogies

Which pattern completes the second pair in the same way as the first pair? Underline the answer.

1
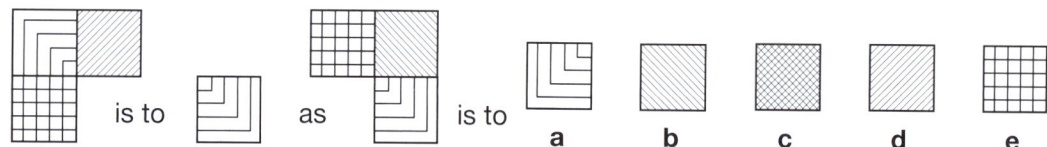

2
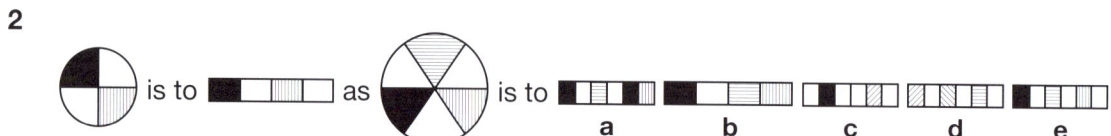

3
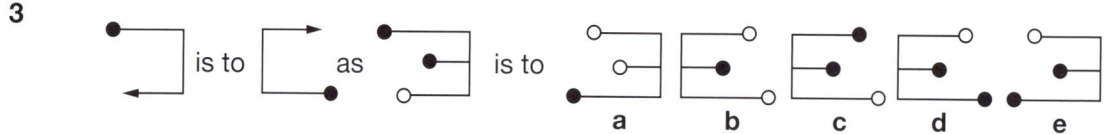

4
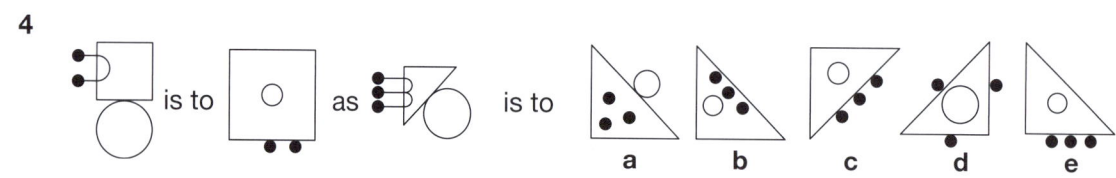

5
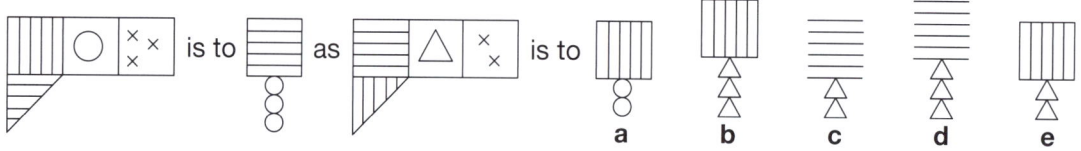

Number types

6 List the prime numbers between 30 and 50.

....

7 Other than 1, what are the common **factors** of these pairs of numbers?

   a 27 and 39   ....

   b 28 and 49   ....

8 What is the smallest **multiple** of 3, 5 and 7?   ....

9 How much greater than 9^3 is 10^3?   ....

Fractions

10 $\frac{2}{3} \times \frac{3}{4} \times 300 =$ ....

> **TOP TIP!**
>
> **When a number is divided by a fraction you turn the fraction upside down, then multiply the two numerators and then multiply the two denominators**

11 What is the value of $\frac{7}{8} \times \frac{4}{5} \div \frac{1}{2}$? Give your answer as a decimal.

....

12 Aunt Agatha has given $\frac{3}{25}$ of her savings to her niece. Then she gives $\frac{4}{5}$ of the remaining savings to her friend. If she had £2000 savings at the start:

   a How much did she give to her niece?   ....

   b How much of her savings did she have left?   ....

Decimals

13 4730.5 ÷ 2.5 = ...

14 104.35 + 29.731 + 0.32 =

....

15 What is 59.46 less than 250.5?

....

16 0.15 × 345.2 = ...

> **TOP TIP!**
> When dividing by a decimal number, move the decimal point to the right in the divisor to give a whole number, and then move the decimal point the same number of places to the right in the number that is being divided or shared out

NVR Reflections and Rotations

17 Which shape on the right is a reflection of the shape on the left? The dotted line shows the line of reflection.

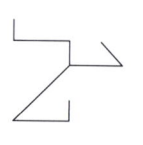  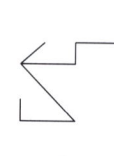 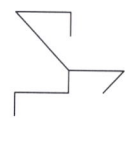 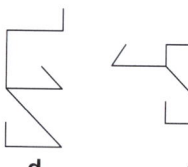 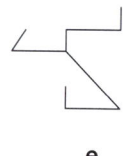

          a   b   c   d   e

18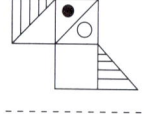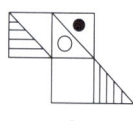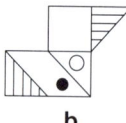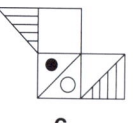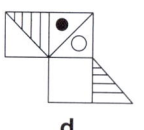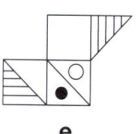

          a   b   c   d   e

19 Which shape on the right is a rotation of the shape on the left?

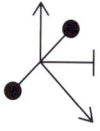 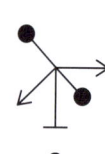 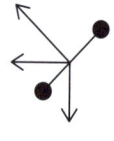 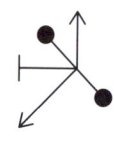 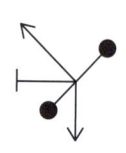 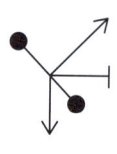

          a   b   c   d   e

20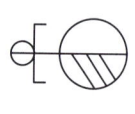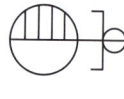

          a   b   c   d   e

BIDMAS

21 $6^2 + 11 + (7 \times 3) - 15 =$ ....

22 $\frac{1}{2} \times (7 + 2^2 + 3^3) =$ ....

23 $(450 \div 5) - (4^2 + 3) =$ ....

24 $(5^3 - 4^3 - 1) \div (3^2 - 2^2) =$ ....

Conversions

25 How many mm are there altogether in 0.02 m, 7.3 cm and 35 mm? ....

26 How many 200 ml bottles can be filled from 5 litres of water? ....

27 2 m + 73 cm + 52 mm = ... mm

28 1010.305 × 1000 = ...

Perimeter, Area and Volume

29 What is the **volume** of a cuboid 16 cm long, 30 mm wide and 10 cm high? ....

30 What is the **perimeter** in cm of a regular decagon with sides of 144 mm? ....

31 How many 50 cm squares are there in a 3 m × 5.5 m rectangle? ....

Properties of Shapes

32 From this diagram, work out the value of the following:

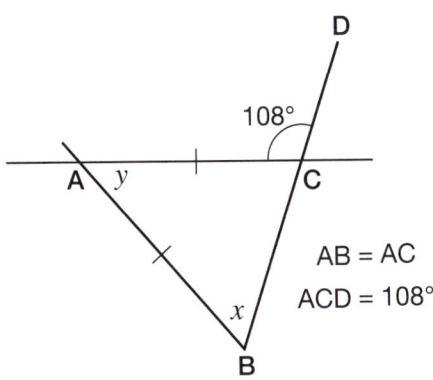

AB = AC
ACD = 108°

a angle x ....

b angle y ....

33 Name the following shapes:

  a Shape with four sides, opposite sides are parallel and no right angles.

  ....

  b Shape with seven sides of equal length.

  ....

Averages

34 A class of 20 children score have an average test score of 42 out 50. The range of their marks is 17, and the lowest score is 29. How many marks above the average were gained by the child with the highest score?

> **TOP TIP!**
>
> When adding a list of numbers in your head, pick out the easy ones first, and put a line through each number as you add it on

....

35 A team played 12 matches. They scored 4 goals in one-third of the matches, 8 goals in a quarter of the matches, 6 goals in 1 match, 2 goals in another, and in 3 matches they did not score. What was their average goal score?

....

36 The speed of ten cars was measured at a fixed point. These are the speeds recorded in kilometres per hour:

45, 50, 58, 48, 35, 51, 49, 50, 45, 49

  a What was the average speed of the ten cars? ....

  b What was range of the speeds measured? ....

Total 40

Mixed Paper 3

Place Value

1 What digits are in the ten thousands column and in the tenths columns of the number five hundred million seven hundred and two thousand and thirty-three point eight nine four?

   ....

2 100 100.01 × 20 = ...

3 Add together the digits in the hundreds column and in the hundredths column of these numbers:

   a 357.36   ....

   b 563.27   ....

4 78.03 × 10^3 = ...

NVR Similar and Different Shapes

Which shape or pattern on the right belongs to the group on the left?
Underline the answer.

5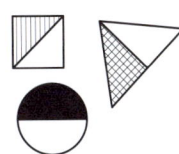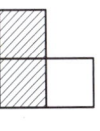

                                         a   b   c   d   e

6

                                         a   b   c   d   e

Which is the odd one out? Underline the answer.

7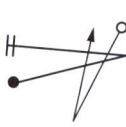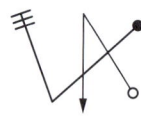

   a   b   c   d   e

8

   a   b   c   d   e

Word and Logic Problems

9 Tom is five years older than Kaz, who is two years younger than Pat. If Pat is seven years old, how old is Tom?

10 In a race the red team are 23 seconds slower than the blue team. The green team are 12 seconds slower than the blue team but 10 seconds faster than the yellow team. Which team came third in the race?

11 There are ten houses in a street. The house numbers are all odd numbers that run on in order, starting at 1. The third and sixth house have green doors. What are the house numbers of the houses with the green doors?

12 At the zoo the seals are fed at 3 p.m. after the monkeys. Feeding the monkeys takes $1\frac{1}{2}$ hours. It takes 20 minutes to weigh out the seals' food, which is done before feeding the monkeys. If the delivery of the seals' food is delayed until 1.30 p.m., what is the earliest time that they can be fed on that day?

Percentages

13 A shoe shop sale is offering 10% discount on everything.

   a In the sale Tracy bought boots for £33 and sandals for £21. How much did she save?

b How much would a pair of slippers be in the sale if they originally cost £30? .....

14 What is 7% of £3200? ....

15 Tickets costing £48 are being sold with a 12.5% discount.
How much will it cost to buy three reduced price tickets? ....

16 Fuel is £1.60 per litre. What is the new price after a 2½% increase? ....

Ratio and Proportion

17 £3000 is shared between three different charities, A, B and C, in the ratio of 1 : 2 : 3.
How much will each charity receive?

A .... **B** .... **C** ....

18 There are 4 ingredients in a fruit cocktail in the ratio of: 2 orange cordial, 2 pineapple cordial, 1 strawberry cordial, 5 lemonade. How many ml of strawberry cordial are needed to make 2½ litres of the cocktail?

....

19 A garden is 75 m long and 22.5 m wide. A plan of the garden is drawn with a scale of 2 cm representing 5 m.

a What is the length of the garden on the plan? ....

b What is the width of the garden on the plan? ....

NVR Codes

20 CMS   BNR   ANT   BMT   ?

CNS	AMR	CNR	ANS	BMS
a	b	c	d	e

21 AL   BM   CM   DN   ?

AN	DL	AM	CL	BN
a	b	c	d	e

22 ADX CEY BFY BDZ ?   AFX AEZ CDZ AFY CFZ
                                a   b   c   d   e

23 ARX BSY BRX ATX ?   ATY BTX BRY ASX ASY
                                a   b   c   d   e

Conversions

24 How many cm are there in 12.4 m, 3.6 cm and 55 mm? ....

25 Convert 5405 seconds into hours, minutes and seconds. ....

26 In a recipe, 2 ounces is converted to 50 g.

   a Convert the following ingredients from ounces to grams.

   4 ounces sugar .... g   6 ounces butter ...... g   8 ounces flour .... g

   b Give the total weight of all the ingredients together in kg. ....

Time

27 What is the time on a digital clock 31 minutes after 23:42? ....

28 What is the time on a digital clock 42 minutes before 3.35 p.m.? ....

29 Station A is 40 km from station B. A train leaves from station A at 10:00 and travels at 30 km per hour towards station B. At what time will it pass a train travelling at the same speed from B to A, which left station B at 10:20?

....

30 A $7\frac{1}{2}$-hour flight lands exactly on time. If it set off at 20:15 local time and its destination is a country where the time zone is 6 hours ahead of the country where it started, what is the local time when it arrives at its destination?

....

Line Graphs

31 This graph shows babies' birth weight for the first three weeks after birth. Use the information on the graph below to answer the questions.

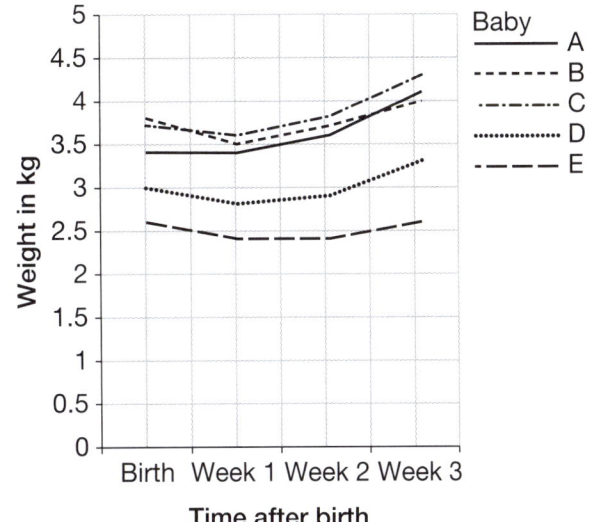

a Which baby made no net gain after three weeks? ....

b Which baby gained the most weight in three weeks? ....

c Which baby lost the most weight in the first week? ....

d Which baby did not lose any weight in the first week? ....

Pie Charts

32 A travel company made a pie chart showing the types of destination that were popular with their customers one year. Complete the table below showing the number of degrees of the pie chart for each location type.

	Number of customers	Angle on pie chart
Beach	50	
Mountains	25	
Lakeside	12	
Cities	23	
Theme parks	10	

Half of the customers who chose beach holidays that year chose lakeside locations the following year. If the other categories stayed the same, by how many degrees will the lakeside section of the pie chart increase when representing the second year?

....

Mixed Paper 4

NVR Sequences and Analogies

Which pattern completes the second pair in the same way as the first pair? Underline the answer.

1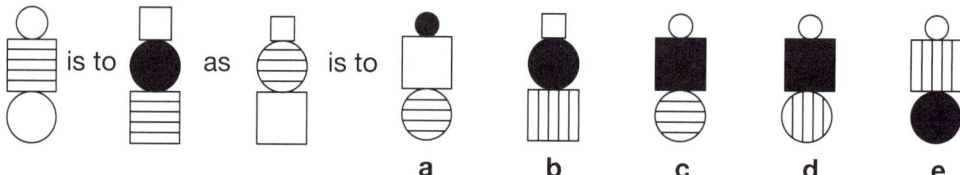

2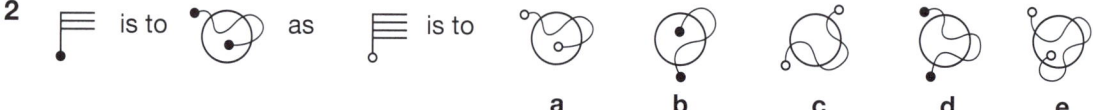

3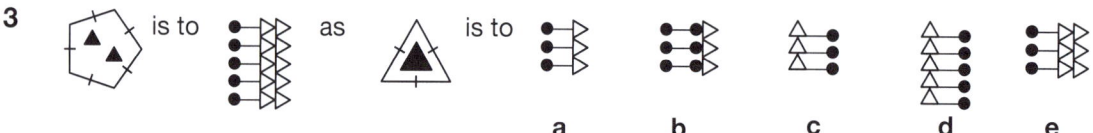

4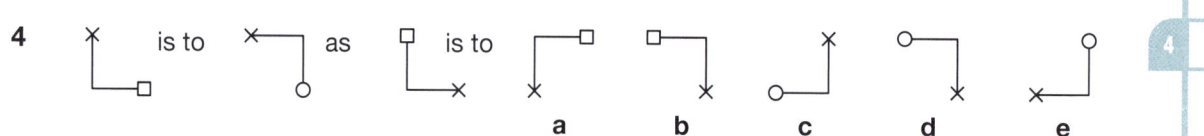

Word and Logic Problems

5 Rosie is 13 days older than Sara, and Sara is 3 days younger than Tasmin. If Tasmin's birthday is 5 June, when is Rosie's birthday? ....

6 In a race, Annie is 3 seconds behind Bella, who is 5 seconds ahead of Carol. Dilma is 1 second ahead of Carol and 4 seconds behind Ellie. In the race, who came in third? ....

7 A runner does a 5 km run by going round a rectangular field five times. If the width of the field is 135 m, what is its length? ....

8   The time between each high tide and each low tide is 6 hours and 20 minutes. On Monday morning high tide is at 05:30. What is the time of the first high tide on Tuesday? ....

Fractions

9   Convert these improper fractions to mixed numbers:

   a $\frac{33}{4}$ ....   b $\frac{13}{5}$ ....

10 $\frac{3}{4} \times \frac{1}{2} \times \frac{2}{3} =$ ....

11 What is $\frac{3}{2}$ of a quarter of 520? ....

12 $\frac{5}{6} + \frac{2}{3} + \frac{1}{4} =$ ....

NVR Grids

Which shape or pattern on the right completes the grid pattern on the left? Underline the answer.

13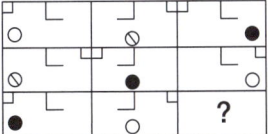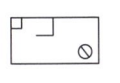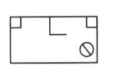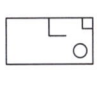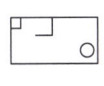
                                                                      a   b   c   d   e

14
                                                                       a   b   c   d   e

15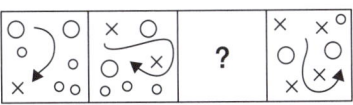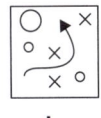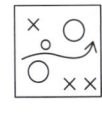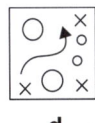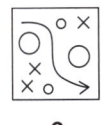
                                                                       a   b   c   d   e

16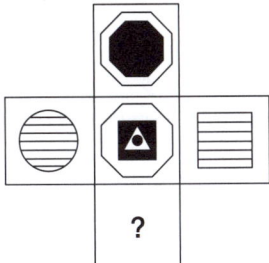
                                                                       a   b   c   d   e

NVR Similar and Different Shapes

Which shape or pattern on the right belongs to the group on the left? Underline the answer.

17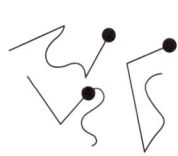

a   b   c   d   e

18

a   b   c   d   e

19

a   b   c   d   e

20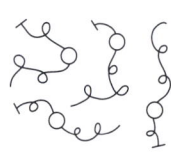

a   b   c   d   e

BIDMAS

21 $(4 \times 3.5) + 7^2 =$ ....

22 $35 + (12 \times 3^2) - 17 =$ ....

23 $(10^3 - 5^3) \div 5 =$ ....

24 $(4^2 + 6) - (63 \div 7) =$ ....

Properties of Shapes

25 Name the following quadrilaterals:

  a Both pairs of opposite sides are parallel and the same length. ....

  b One pair of adjacent sides is equal in length, and the opposite pair is equal but a different length from the first pair ....

26 On a regular hexagonal prism, state the number of:

a faces .... b edges ....

NVR Nets

27 Which cube can be made from the net on the left? Underline the answer.

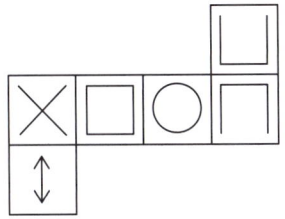  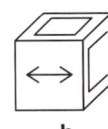 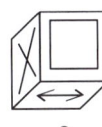  
                                  a   b   c   d   e

28 Which cube cannot be made from the net on the left? Underline the answer.

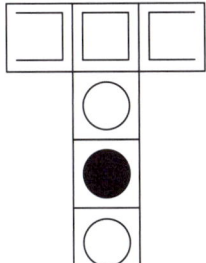  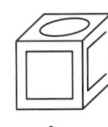 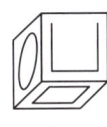  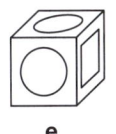
                                  a   b   c   d   e

29

                                  a   b   c   d   e

30 Which cube on the right can be made from the net on the left? Underline the answer.

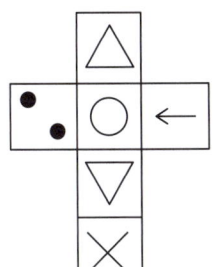  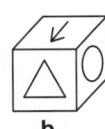  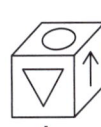 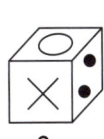
                                  a   b   c   d   e

Line graphs

31 Three children plant beans on the same day. After one week, there is still no growth. After two weeks, the beans have germinated and are growing.

The height of each plant is recorded on this graph.

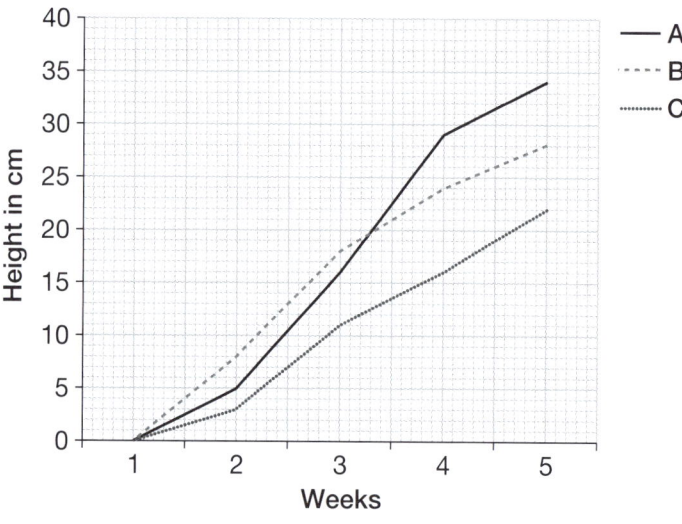

a What was the difference in height between the plant that was the tallest and the one that was the shortest at three weeks?

....

b How tall was plant C after four weeks? ....

c What is the combined height in cm of plant A and plant B after five weeks? ......

d How much taller is plant B than plant C after two weeks? ....

Pie Charts

32 Forty children were asked what their favourite ice cream flavour was and the results are shown on the pie chart.

a Which was the least favourite flavour? ....

b If 12 of the 40 children chose blueberry, how many degrees is the sector representing blueberry? ....

Finished these Mixed Papers? Go online at www.bond11plus.co.uk and register for FREE RESOURCES to get two additional Mixed Papers.

Curveball Questions 2

1 Mr Stone travels at 45 km per hour from Alderly to Benton, a distance of 90 km. Mr Price travels at 60 km per hour from Benton to Alderly. Mr Stone leaves Alderly at 9 a.m.

    a What time must Mr Price leave Benton to meet Mr Stone halfway between Alderly and Benton? ....

    b What time will Mr Price then arrive at Alderly? ....

2 Sammi's dance class is a 20-minute drive from home. Her sister Charlie's gym class is only 15 minutes away from home. The gym class is 10 minutes from the dance class venue. Both classes are on the same day. The dance class starts at 9 a.m. and the gym class starts at 10 a.m.

    a If their mother takes Sammi to dance class arriving on time and then goes back home to get Charlie, how long will she have at home before leaving to take Charlie to the gym class?

    ....

    b If she stays to watch the gym class before going to fetch Sammi after her $1\frac{1}{2}$-hour dance class, how long can the mother watch Charlie at the gym class?

    ....

3 Complete the following table by identifying the number sequence.

A	B	C	D	E	F	G	H	I	J	K	L	M	N	O	P	R	S	T	W
1	2	4	7		16	22		37	46	56		79	92	106	121		154	172	191

    a Decode this message: 2 : 137 : 37 : 92 : 22   16 : 106 : 106 : 7

    ....

    b Put this message into code: CALL SAM NOW

    ....

Test Papers

Test Paper 1

> **TOP TIP!**
> With full-length test papers, work carefully and systematically through the paper reading the questions very carefully. Do not be tempted to rush, but also do not spend too long on one question if you get stuck as you can always come back to it at the end if there is time.

Which pattern on the right completes the second pair in the same way as the first pair? Underline the answer.

1  is to as  is to
                                                            a   **b**   **c**   **d**   **e**

2 is to  as is to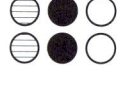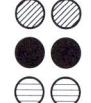
                                            a   **b**   **c**   **d**   **e**

3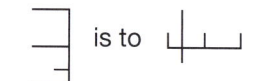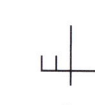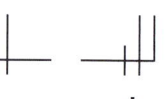
                                            a   **b**   **c**   **d**   **e**

4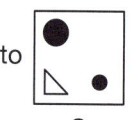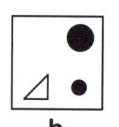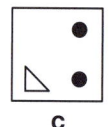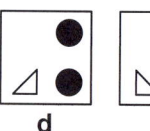
                                            a   **b**   **c**   **d**   **e**

5 Give 2 factors other than 1 that are common to 12, 28 and 84. ....

6 Which of the following numbers are not multiples of 3 and 7W? Circle them.

    21   33   42   49   63   81

7 Which numbers less than 10 are prime numbers? ....

8 Fifteen houses in a street have even numbers starting at number 10. They decide to paint their doors alternately in yellow, blue and white. If the fifth house wants to be yellow, what colour door will house number 28 have?

....

9 Doug uses 3 litres of water a day from the garden tank for his greenhouse. The tank holds 150 litres. If the tank is full on Monday, and three days later it gains another 2 litres from a shower of rain, how many litres will be in the tank 2 weeks later if it does not rain again?

....

10 Five children enter a competition to grow the tallest sunflower. Abi's flower is taller than Harjit's but 5 cm shorted than Ben's which is taller than Amy's. Toni's flower is 11 cm taller than Abi's. Whose sunflower is the tallest?

....

11 $(\frac{3}{4} \times \frac{3}{4}) + \frac{3}{8} - \frac{9}{12} =$ ....

12 What is the value of $\frac{5}{7} + \frac{3}{14} + 1\frac{1}{2}$?
Give your answer as a mixed number. ....

13 $\frac{42}{4} \div \frac{6}{2} =$ ....

14 $\frac{1}{2} + \frac{1}{4} + \frac{2}{3} + \frac{5}{6} =$ ....

15 What is the difference between 40% of 750 and 30% of 620? ....

16 The price of a house valued at £375 000 goes up 4% over 2 years. What is its value after 2 years?

....

17 If 12% tax has to be paid on profit, what tax must a shopkeeper pay if one year he spends £760 000 on goods which he sells for a total of £1 245 000?

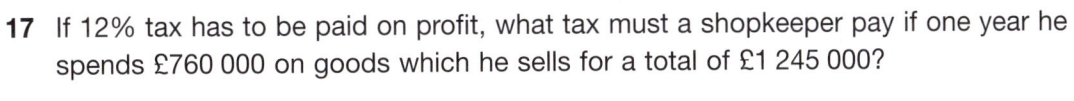

Which shape on the right is a reflection of the shape on the left?
Underline the answer.

18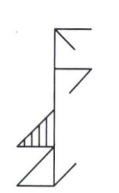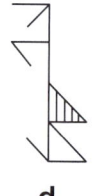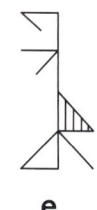

                                        a   b   c   d   e

19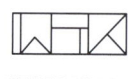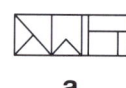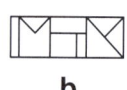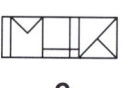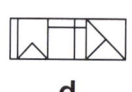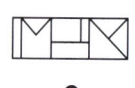

                                        a   b   c   d   e

Which shape on the right is a rotation of the shape on the left?
Underline the answer.

20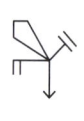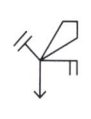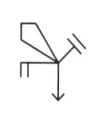

                                        a   b   c   d   e

21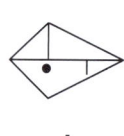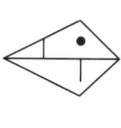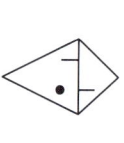

                                        a   b   c   d   e

22 Mabel leaves £13 920 in her will to be shared with her 5 grandchildren in the ratio of 1 : 2 : 2 : 3 : 4. How much will they each receive?

....

23 A scale plan of a garden is drawn up with 1 m represented by 2 cm on the plan. If the rectangular flowerbed is 6.3 cm wide and 9 cm long on the plan, what are its actual measurements?

....

24 The proportion of fruit puree to water to sugar for making jam is 2 : 1 : 4. If the fruit puree and water together weigh 4.2 kg, what weight of sugar is required?

....

25 Pascal has three uncles, their ages are 45, 53 and 58. Pascal's age is half of their average age, how old is Pascal?

....

26 State what comes next:

   a 4280, 2140, 1070, 535, ...   **b** 1.1, 4.3, 7.5, 10.7, ...

27 $10^2 \times 0.0218 \times 10^3 \times 0.3 =$ ....

28 Underline the odd one out:

   $\frac{1}{8}$ 12.5% $\frac{3}{32}$ $\frac{5}{40}$ 0.125

29 $(8^2 \times 2) + (6^2 - 2^2) - 55 =$ ....

30 $4^3 + 3^3 - 2^3 =$ ....

31 $4024 \div 2^2 \times 10^3 =$ ....

32 $(5^3 - 7^2) \times 10^2 \div 5 =$ ....

33 Express 4 053 867 mm in km, m and cm. ....

34 If 1 ml of water weighs 1 g, what is the total weight of a metal tank containing 1000 litres of water if the tank weighs 30 kg? ....

35 Some children tried to work out how many seconds there are in a week and got several different answers. Underline the correct answer.

   A 6 400 800 s   **B** 604 800 s   **C** 6 040 000 s   **D** 640 000

36 The height of a right-angled triangle is 4 cm and its base is 10 cm. What is its area?

....

37 What is the total surface area of a box 50 cm long, 30 cm high and 25 cm wide?

....

Use the following train timetable to answer questions 38–41.

	Train A	Train B	Train C	Train D
Acton	09:05	11:10	15:45	18:10
Beaston	09:43	12:04	16:52	18:38
Colbridge	10:10	12:31	17:21	19:15
Dundry	10:38	13:07	17:57	20:00

38 How much more time does it take for train C to go from Acton to Colbridge than it does for train A? ....

39 A passenger arrives at Beaston at 14:30. How long must he wait to get a train to Dundry? ....

40 Which train has the shortest travel time from Acton to Beaston? ....

41 One day all trains between Acton and Beaston are delayed by 14 minutes, and then leave five minutes late for the onward journey to Colbridge. At what time will train B now arrive at Colbridge?

....

42 What shapes have the following?

   a Four sides and one pair of parallel sides. ....

   b Two pairs of parallel sides of equal lengths and four right angles. ....

   c Three sides all of different lengths. ....

   d Five equal sides. ....

43 What 3-D shape has four equal triangular faces and four vertices?

....

44 What is the total length of all of the edges of a cuboid which is 6 cm long, 4 cm wide and 5 cm high?

....

45 A ship sails the following course, with all turns made in a clockwise direction. In which direction is it travelling at the end?

Setting off North – 45 degrees – 135 degrees – 90 degrees – 45 degrees

....

46 Donna walks along a road in a westerly direction. She takes the second turning left, the first right, then goes all the way along that road, turning right at the end. Assuming that all of the turns are right angles, in what direction is she facing at the end?

....

47 A clock starts at midday with both hands in a vertical position.

  a When the time is 2.30 p.m., through how many degrees has the small hand moved?

  ....

  b When the time is 2.30 p.m., through how many degrees has the big hand turned?

  ....

48 A lighthouse is 5 km due north of a rocky island and 5 km due west of the harbour wall. What direction would you go in to travel from the harbour wall to the island?

....

49 Class 2 recorded the daily temperature every day for two weeks, at the same time and in the same place. Their results are recorded in this graph.

  a If the mean daily temperature for that time of year is 18°C, which days in Week 2 exceeded the mean?

  ....

  b What was the average daily temperature for Week 2?

  ....

c What was the difference in temperature between the following?

  i The hottest day in Week 1 and the coolest day in Week 2? ....

  ii The hottest day in Week 2 and the coolest day in Week 1? ....

50 The stopping distance of a moving car from when a hazard appears to the point when it stops is made up of the 'thinking distance' and the 'braking distance'. This table shows these distances for cars when travelling at different speeds.

Speed of travel	Thinking distance	Braking distance
20 mph	6 m	6 m
30 mph	9 m	14 m
40 mph	12 m	24 m
50 mph	15 m	38 m
60 mph	18 m	55 m
70 mph	21 m	75 m

a What is the total stopping distance for a car travelling at 60 mph? ....

b How much greater is the braking distance when travelling at 70 mph than 30 mph?

....

c How much longer is the total stopping distance when travelling at 40 mph than 30 mph?

....

d How many times longer is the total stopping distance at 70 mph compared to 20 mph?

....

e In wet weather all braking distances are twice as long. To be able to brake within 48 m, what is the maximum travelling speed?

....

51 In a bag of mixed sweets the number of red sweets varies. Six bags were checked and the number of red sweets were recorded as follows:

17   15   18   13   11   16

What was the average number of red sweets? ....

52 Three test scores together had an average of 86%. If one score was 78% and another score was 90%, what was the third score?

....

53 Here is the price of each of the last five bicycles sold in a bike shop:

£56   £99   £40   £140   £120

a What was the average price of the bicycles sold? ....

b The two cheaper bicycles were on special offer with £25 off. If a similar set of 5 bicycles is sold the next week, and the offer has ended, what will the new average price be?

....

54 In a school of 350 pupils there were 12 classes. Five classes had 31 pupils, 4 classes had 28 pupils, 2 classes had 27 pupils, and the rest were in the twelfth class.

a How many pupils were in the twelfth class? ....

b What was the average class size rounded to the nearest whole number? ....

55 In a café ten customers buy afternoon tea. Three spend £12.50 each, three spend £11 each and one spends £28 for the four of them. What was the average price of afternoon tea for these ten customers?

....

56 A class of 30 children all have refreshments at the theatre. The average cost per child is £2.10. The teacher pays with four £20 notes. What change does she get?

....

Total **70**

Test Paper 2

1 $0.0023 \times 10^3 \times 200 = $ ....

2 What is the total of the digits in the ten thousands column, the tens column and the tenths column in each of these numbers?

a 4 638 674.842 .... **b** 850 376.673 ....

3 Write in digits the number one hundred and one million, eleven thousand, one hundred and eleven. ....

4 What number is one million times greater than 0.00047? ....

Which shape on the right belongs to the group of shapes on the left?
Underline the answer.

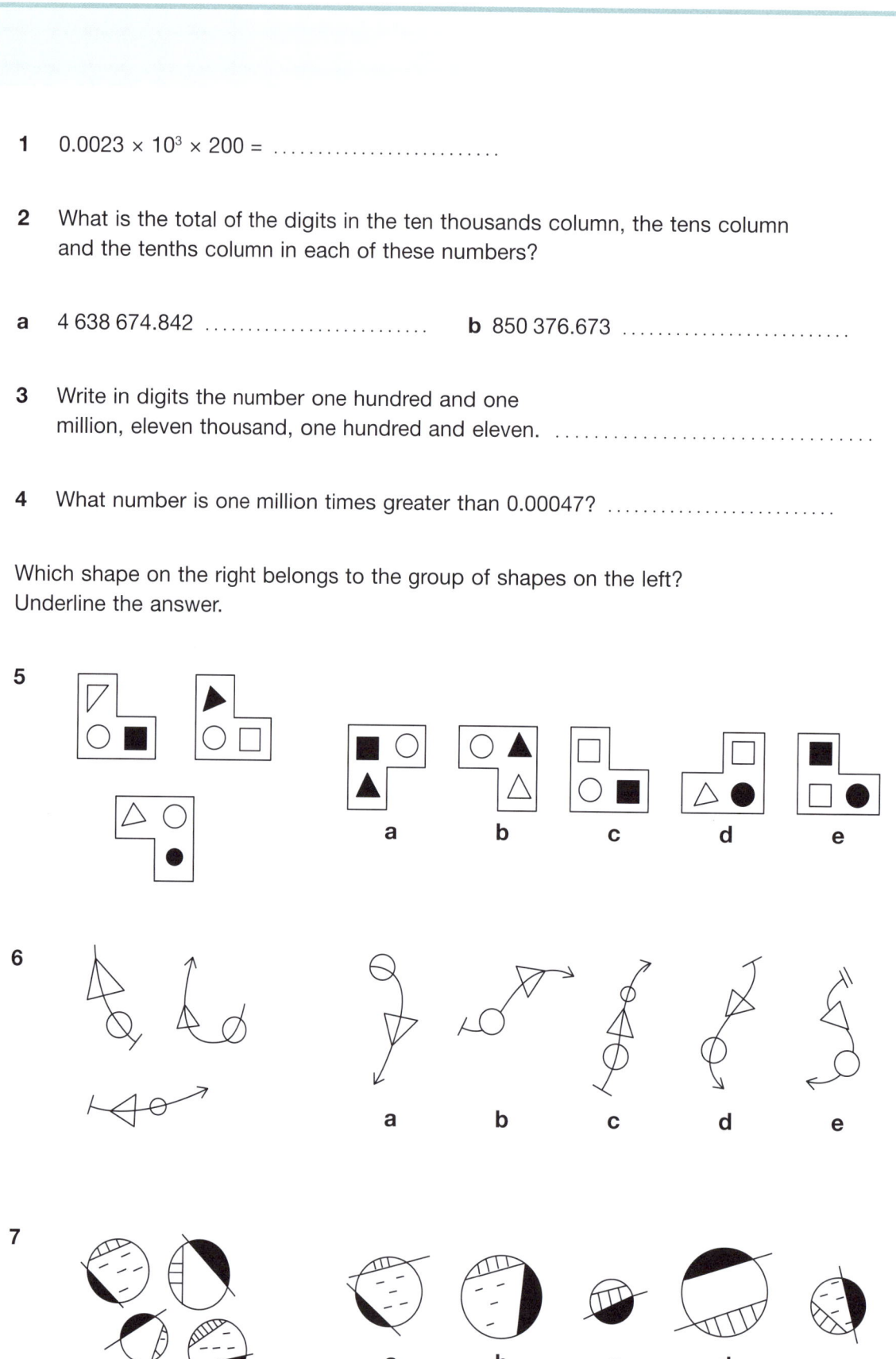

8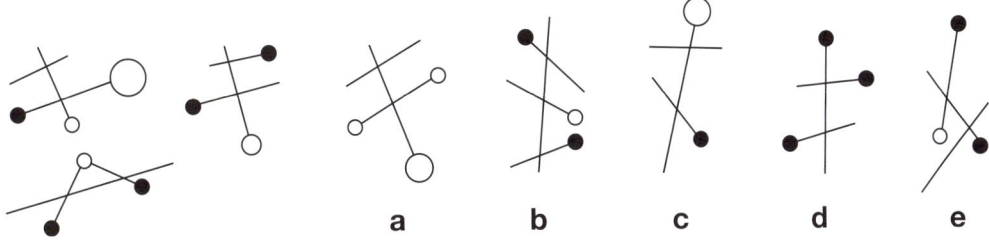

a   b   c   d   e

9 Jit won a race with his friends. He was 4 seconds faster than Ben, who was 7 seconds faster than Connor. Anya was 13 seconds faster than Matt. If Connor took 48 seconds, what were the times of the other runners?

Jit .... Anya .... Matt ....

10 A hosepipe is on for two hours to fill a paddling pool. The pool takes 80 litres of water. After the children have been playing there are only 75 litres left. How long will it take to top up the pool to 80 litres again if water flows through the hosepipe at the same rate as before?

....

11 A journey which normally takes two hours is slower than usual due to roadworks along one-quarter of the journey. The roadworks halve the driver's usual speed. How long will the journey take?

....

12 A is hotter than B, and C is colder than D, D is hotter than A, B is colder than C. Which of these cannot be true? Underline the answer.

   a A is hotter than C.   **b** D is colder than B.   **c** C is hotter than A.

13 $0.125 \times 3.5 = $ ....

14 $753.72 + 9.357 + 100.003 = $ ....

15 $1101.101 \times $ .... $\times 5 = $ five million five hundred and five thousand, five hundred and five

16 $4000 \div $ .... $= 62.5$

Which pattern completes the larger shape or grid? Underline the answer.

17

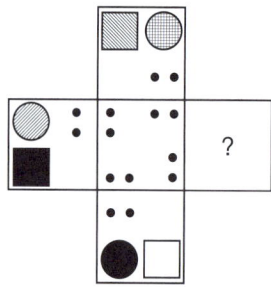 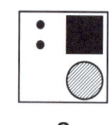 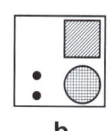  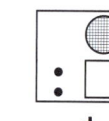 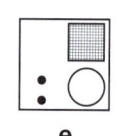
a b c d e

18

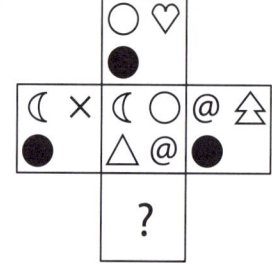  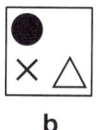   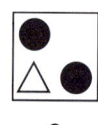
a b c d e

19

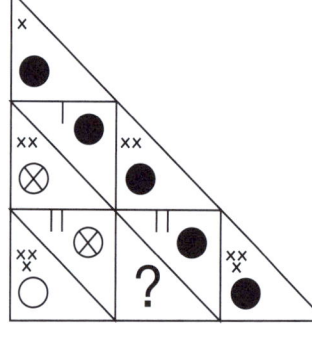 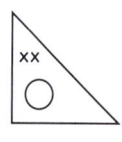 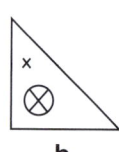 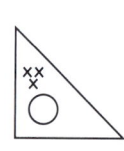 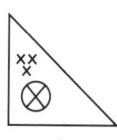 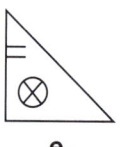
a b c d e

20

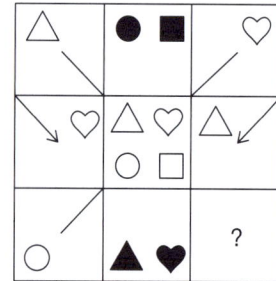 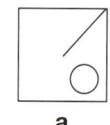 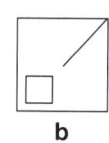 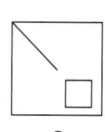 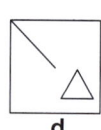 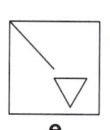
a b c d e

21

a b c d e

22 If £66 350 is shared between Vicky, Rob and Sue in the ratio of 1 : 3 : 4, how much do they each get?

Vicky .... Rob .... Sue ....

23 Pat has enough money to buy 42 bulbs for the garden. He wants to have three colours, red, white and blue, in the ratio of 1 : 2 : 3. How many of each colour should he buy?

....

24 A gardener needs to make some concrete for the garden fence posts. The concrete mixture has cement, fine sand, coarse sand in the ratio of 1 : 2 : 4. If she uses 3 kg of fine sand, how much cement and coarse sand are needed?

....

25 $3x^2 + 25 = 100$ $x = $ ....

26 Look at the first two triplets to work out the pattern, then complete the third triplet.

a 12 (24) 2   4 (28) 7   3 (39) ....

b 4 (13) 9   17 (28) 11   23 (........................) 8

c 48 (16) 3   75 (25) 3   .... (17) 3

27 $7^2 + (3 \times 2^3) - 4^2 = $ ....

28 $\frac{1}{2} \times 56 + 108 \div 12 - 20 = $ ....

29 $3490 \div 10^2 \times 2^2 = $ ....

30 $83 + 5 \times 9 - 8^2 = $ ....

Which code matches the shape or pattern given at the end of each line?
Underline the answer.

31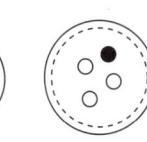

ADX   CEX   BFZ   AGY   ?

BDZ	CFY	CGX	BEY	AEY
a	b	c	d	e

32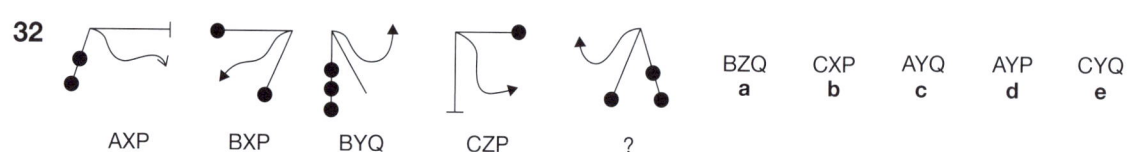

	BZQ	CXP	AYQ	AYP	CYQ
	a	b	c	d	e

AXP　　BXP　　BYQ　　CZP　　?

33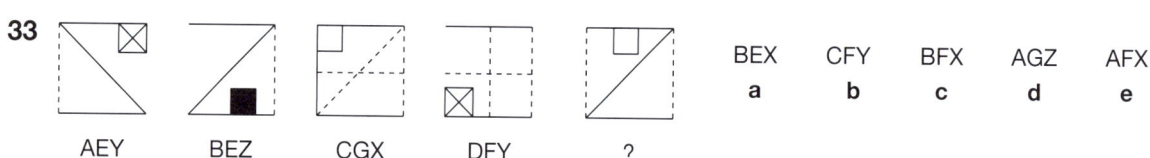

	BEX	CFY	BFX	AGZ	AFX
	a	b	c	d	e

AEY　　BEZ　　CGX　　DFY　　?

34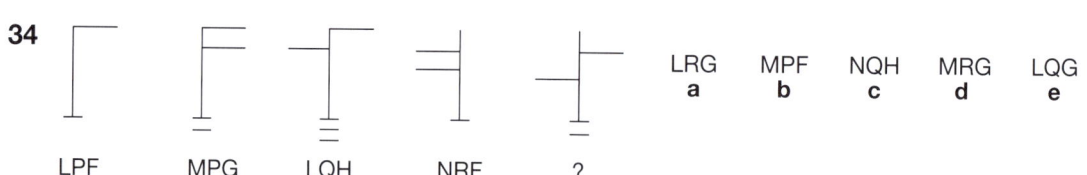

	LRG	MPF	NQH	MRG	LQG
	a	b	c	d	e

LPF　　MPG　　LQH　　NRF　　?

35 What is the total surface area of the four largest faces in a cuboid measuring 5 cm by 10 cm by cm?

....

36 How many small bricks measuring 10 cm × 10 cm × 20 cm will fit into a crate that is 1 m long, 40 cm wide and 40 cm high?

....

37 The diagram below shows the dimensions of a new lounge area and a corridor in a hotel. How many square metres of flooring will it require?

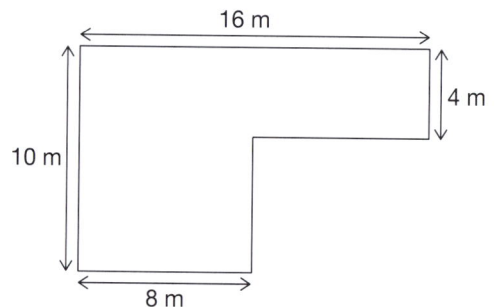

....

38 If a quarter of the distance around a hexagonal running track is 1200 m, what is the length of each side of the hexagon?

....

39 If a car is travelling at 60 miles per hour, how long will it take to cover 135 miles?

....

40 Complete the following table giving the times in 24-hour clock notation.

	Quarter past midnight	4.55 a.m.	Midday	3.30 p.m.	9.45 p.m.	Ten to midnight
24-hour clock						

41 The 7.10 a.m. train to London is running 17 minutes late. The journey takes 1 hour 42 minutes. When will it arrive?

....

42 How many minutes are there altogether in 1 week, 1 day and 1 hour?

....

43

    a If angle x is 54°, what is the size of angle y? ....

    b ABF and CDE are both triangles, what type of triangles are they?

    ABF ....   CDE ....

44 How many pairs of parallel lines are there in a regular octagon? ....

45 How many straight and how many curved edges do each of these 3-D solid shapes have?

   a cube ....   **b** triangular-based pyramid ....

   c cylinder ....   **d** cone ....

46 Which cube cannot be made from the following net? Underline the answer.

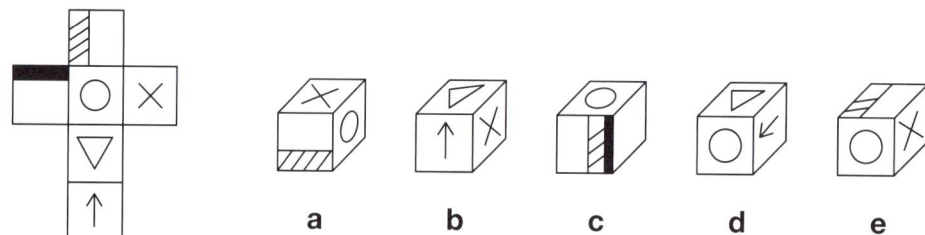

a   **b**   **c**   **d**   **e**

47 Which cube cannot be made from the following net? Underline the answer.

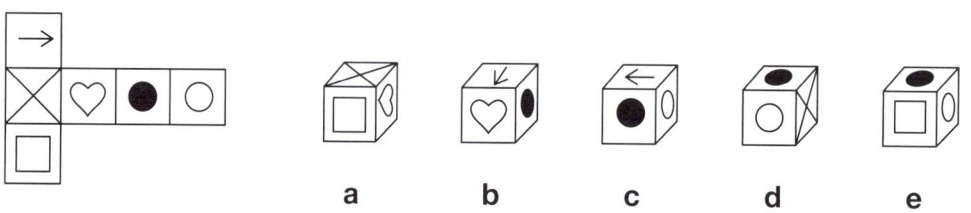

a   **b**   **c**   **d**   **e**

48 Which cube can be made from the following net? Underline the answer.

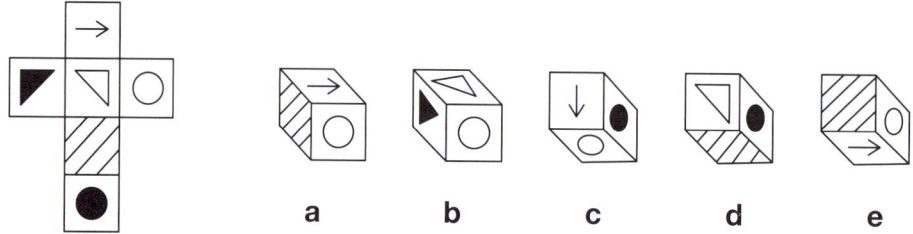

a   **b**   **c**   **d**   **e**

49 Which cube can be made from the following net? Underline the answer.

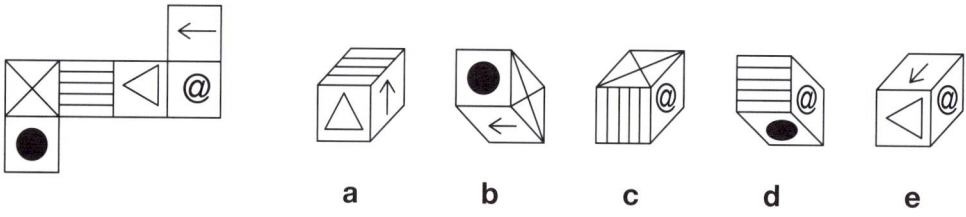

a   **b**   **c**   **d**   **e**

50 A hall was decorated with many different-coloured balloons. The number of balloons of each colour was recorded on a graph.

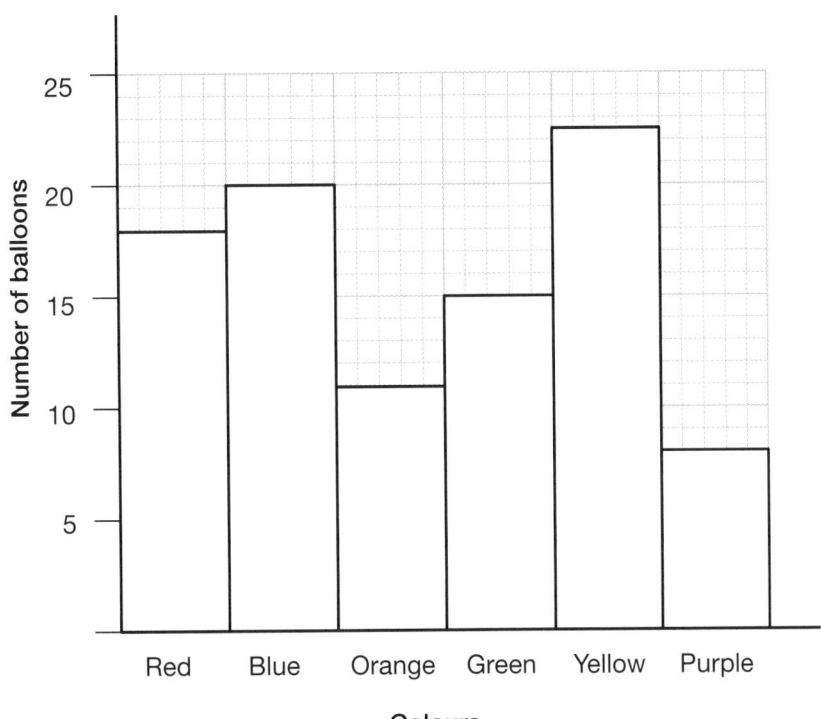

a How many balloons in total were used?

....

b How many more yellow than orange balloons were there?

....

c How many more balloons of what colour need to be bought to make sure that there are at least 15 balloons of each colour?

....

d There are five more blue balloons than the number of Anya's favourite-colour balloons. What is her favourite colour?

....

51 Kalim carried out a traffic survey outside his home for an hour and recorded what he saw on a bar graph.

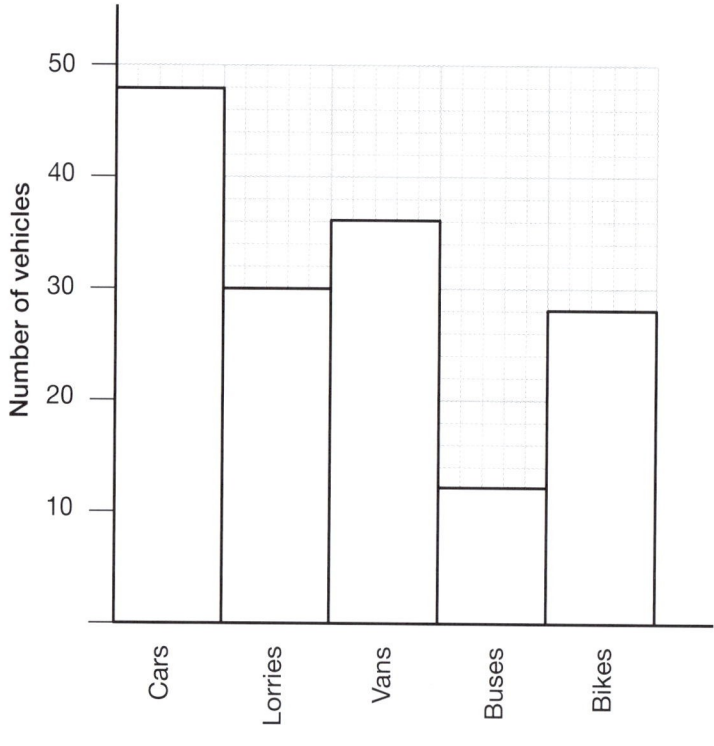

a How many more vans than lorries were there?

....

b What fraction of all the vehicles recorded were cars?

....

c If one-third of all the traffic was travelling into town and the rest was leaving town, how many vans were travelling into town during the hour that Kalim was recording?

....

52 A library records the types of books that were taken out during one day. Put the results from the table below into a bar graph.

Children's fiction	Children's non-fiction	Travel	Biographies	Adult fiction	Cookery	Hobbies
42	26	38	31	53	10	25

a Choose an appropriate scale for the x axis and label it.

b How many more:

  i adult fiction books than children's fiction books were taken out that day?

  ....

  ii travel books than cookery books were taken out that day?

  ....

53 The results of a questionnaire completed by 200 attendees on a course are shown as percentages in this table, with Grade 1 being excellent and Grade 5 being very poor. Results are shown as a percentage.

	Grade 1	Grade 2	Grade 3	Grade 4	Grade 5
Quality of speakers	37	58	5	0	0
Choice of topics covered	54	44	2	0	0
Convenience of location	12	25	33	24	6
Quality of refreshments	82	16	2	0	0
Usefulness of handouts	0	17	61	17	5

a How many people thought the quality of the speakers was excellent?

b Which question had the widest spread of opinions?

c Which question had the second-highest proportion of excellent grades?

d If results for Grades 1 and 2 are combined as 'better grades', and results for Grades 4 and 5 are combined as 'poorer grades', how many more people gave better grades than poorer grades for the convenience of the location?

54 Here is the annual average rainfall and temperature from an Egyptian weather station.

	Jan	Feb	Mar	Apr	May	Jun	Jul	Aug	Sep	Oct	Nov	Dec
Rain (mm)	92	94	124	120	129	82	81	88	101	76	118	114
Average temp (°C)	2.8	5.3	10.3	16.2	20.8	25.6	27.5	26.1	22.2	16.4	10	4.7

a Which is the wettest month?

b On average, how many more mm of rain were there in the wettest month than the driest month?

....

c What is the average temperature across the three months of Sep, Oct and Nov?

....

d What is the temperature range between the hottest and the coolest month?

....

e Between which months is the average temperature difference less than 2 degrees?

....

55 Polly collected data about pupils' favourite colours. She wants to show the data on a pie chart.

a Complete the table, working out how many degrees must be given to each colour.

	Yellow	Orange	Red	Purple	Blue	Green
	7	2	9	3	5	4
No. of degrees on pie chart						

b If half of the greens join the purples and half join the reds, what are the new sector sizes for purple and red?

....

Total 80

Keywords

Some special words and symbols are used in this book. You will find them in bold the first time they appear. These words are explained here.

area	the surface or amount of two-dimensional space taken up by a shape or object, also written as cm^2
average	to find the average of two or more numbers, you add the values together and divide by the number of values
coordinate	a pair of numbers used to locate a point. The first number is the distance along the horizontal line and the second number is the distance along the vertical line
cube	a regular 3-dimensional solid shape where every face is an identical square and every angle a right angle
cuboid	a 3-dimensional solid shape where each surface is a rectangle (includes squares) and every angle is a right angle
degrees	1 the unit of measurement for temperature 2 the unit of measurement of angle, with 360 degrees making one complete turn The symbol ° can be used instead of the word 'degrees'
difference	to find the difference between two numbers, take the smaller number away from the larger number
digit	any of the numerals 0,1, 2, 3, 4, 5, 6, 7, 8, 9
equilateral	a triangle with all sides the same length
even	numbers which are exactly divisible by 2 are even
factor	a factor of a number is a whole number which divides exactly into another larger number, e.g. the factors of 8 are 1, 2, 4 and 8
heptagon	a polygon that has 7 interior angles and 7 sides
hexagon	a polygon that has 6 interior angles and 6 sides
kite	a quadrilateral with two pairs of adjoining sides the same length
mean	the average of a set of quantitative data, found by totalling the individual quantities and then dividing by the number of quantities in the set
minimum	the lowest value
multiple	a whole number that is the product of another number is one of its multiples
nearest ten	where the first number 'dropped off' is 5 or more, the number in the next column is rounded up, e.g. 375 to the nearest ten becomes 380

odd	numbers that are not exactly divisible by 2
parallel	two lines are parallel when they are equidistant along their entire length
parallelogram	a quadrilateral with opposite sides parallel
percentage	indicates hundredths, e.g. 5% is $\frac{5}{100}$
perimeter	the distance around the edge of a shape
pie chart	a circle where sectors are marked with their areas representing the proportion of that part of a group of categories
prism	a shape which has the same section all the way through, e.g. a 'tent' shape is a triangular prism
quadrilateral	any polygon with four sides and four interior angles
range	the difference between the largest and the smallest value in a set of numbers
ratio	division of a quantity into parts that are in a fixed proportion to each other, e.g. in a ratio of 1 : 2, the second quantity will be twice the size of the first quantity
rhombus	quadrilateral with all four sides the same length, a square is a special type of rhombus
rounding	the process of approximating a number to a given degree of accuracy
series	set of numbers where there is a pattern determining the difference between each term of the series (also called a sequence)
speed	the measure of distance travelled in a given amount of time. Its units will have a unit of length per unit of time, e.g. km per hour
total	the sum of a number of values all added together
volume	the space taken up by a solid object
x **axis**	the name given to the horizontal line going across a graph
y **axis**	the name given to the vertical line going up along a graph

11+ Study Guide

Essentials

- Don't worry too much about the level that you start at. Beginning with an easier book can help your confidence
- Make sure you have the right equipment – you will need your pencils, an eraser, and a notebook
- This book contains skills guidance and worked examples, but if you need more help with technique, the Bond Handbooks might also be useful to you.

Studying Effectively

1. Turn to the first topic and read the Key Skills box. You might want to read it a few times or with someone else to understand it properly or to underline key words.

2. Read the worked example a few times and make sure you understand it.

3. In your notebook, write down the topic heading and the worked example on a new page. This is for you to revise and remember. Once you have completed the final book, you will have a super-useful notebook that you can use in secondary school.

4. Now set a timer – a kitchen timer, a watch or phone with an alarm – for the timed section.

5. Work your way through the questions carefully. If you don't know the answer to something, draw a circle around the question number and take your best guess. This is important as you can find patterns if you make mistakes and it highlights where you need to consolidate.

6. Ask someone to mark the paper for you or mark it yourself and see where you made mistakes. Is there a common pattern? For every mistake, decide if it is not knowing the technique properly, not consolidating the technique enough or a loss of focus and label this next to each question using T = technique, C = consolidation, F = focus.

7. Have another go at the questions you made errors in to understand what you did wrong. If it is vocabulary problem, write down the word with its meaning / synonym / antonym at the back of your book so that you widen your vocabulary range.

Making Mistakes

Everyone makes mistakes and they are an important part of how we learn. The reason we practise before an exam is so that we can make those mistakes in a safe space rather than in the test itself and that way we can learn from them and make fewer mistakes when it really matters.

Remember that there is no such thing as a 'silly mistake'. You are not silly, and neither is your mistake. It is usually not understanding the technique, not consolidating the skill needed so that it is only partially remembered, or you have lost focus. Losing focus does not mean that you have done something bad, it just means that your attention was on something else. These tips can help:

Not Understanding the Technique:

- Go back to the learning section and reread the key skills box
- Look at the worked example that you have in your notebook
- Use the Bond Handbook for more support.

Not Consolidating Enough:

- It is amazing how much consolidation is needed by everyone so don't worry about doing lots of additional questions
- Look at Bond online for some more questions to help you revise
- Ask someone to test you on the technique.

Losing Focus:

- Make sure that you are not too tired, hungry, thirsty or distracted
- Work out where you have made a mistake and break it down into sections. It might be that you focus on tricky division, but go too fast when it comes to addition. It might be that you read the comprehension extract, but you lost focus and misread it
- Once you have identified the problem area, make sure that in new questions, you check yourself and focus carefully.

Common Problems

'I don't have time to study.'

Make sure that you have a timetable that is doable. If you have lots of activities that take up time, perhaps break your work up. The books all have timing sections so fit in smaller sections when you can. It's important to talk to your parent if you feel that you need more time for your 11+ work.

'I find it hard to complete my homework as I want to play instead.'

Motivation is difficult for most people. Don't completely stop all fun activities during the 11+ but get a balance. Key to this is a timetable so you know when, what and where to study. Make sure it is doable and build in something fun if you complete your homework for the day. Another tip is to write down your reasons for doing the 11+. Whether it is for your own personal sense of achievement, keeping your family happy, getting into the school your friends are going to, or even that the school is just more convenient, understanding how important each of those reasons is for you and focussing on that can help you to commit the time required to make it happen. If you can't find strong enough reasons for committing the time, perhaps talk with your family about it.

'My friend is using different books to me.'

The Bond 11+ system covers English/Verbal Reasoning and Maths/Non-verbal reasoning/spatial awareness. Bond has had many decades of success in 11+ material. Many tutors will only use Bond for their pupils, and they get an exceptionally high pass rate. It doesn't mean that Bond is the only 11+ provider, so don't worry that your friend is using different material. What is important is that you are fully prepared for your CEM online exam, and you can have confidence in the Bond system.

'I'm scared of failing.'

It is natural to feel that. Remember that you cannot climb a mountain in one gigantic step. You need lots and lots of little steps to get to the top. The 11+ is like that. You can't sit down and learn everything straight away, but the little steps you take will lead you to the exam. Remember that every mistake can be identified and once you identify it, you may be able to understand it and solve the problem for next time. Mistakes are perfection in progress! If a selective school is the best learning environment for you, then you can work little and often through the books and then test papers leading up to the exam. If you find it too much and you are working at your full potential already, then maybe a school that is not selective will suit your learning better. There is no 'best school' and 'worst school' for everyone. It is the best school for an individual child. Do talk to someone about your feelings though as you need to feel supported.

'My friend has a tutor. Do I need one?'

Whether or not to have tutor depends on many different factors, including where your particular strengths and challenges lie, your own approach to learning, and whether your parents are comfortable with the costs involved. The Bond system is rigorous and aims to support every child with a range of books and learning materials. The Bond Handbooks can do the job of a tutor and many tutors also use the Bond books and Handbooks with their pupils. Bond has been providing 11+ material since the 1960s, helping thousands of pupils to pass their 11+ exams without having a tutor.

'I don't want to do the 11+ exam.'

This is a conversation to have with your family, but the best advice might be to follow the 11+ books anyway. They will teach you skills, techniques and methods that will give you self-confidence regardless of the secondary school you attend. No knowledge is a waste, and you will be keeping your options open.

There is more information on the Bond website. Bond has a Parent's Guide to the 11+ and there is a range of supportive printed and online material. See online for further details: www.bond11plus.co.uk

Answers

Learning Paper 1: Special Numbers, Place Value and Sequences

1 **c** The right angle corner of the larger L-shape of these patterns is in the same corner for two terms then rotates 90° clockwise for the following two terms, so the next term in the sequence will have the larger L-shape right angle in the bottom right corner of the shape, which eliminates options a and e. The shorter line at the end of one arm alternates between being at 45° and 90°, always directed away from the L-shape, so the next shape will have the short line at 45° outwards.

2 **e** Alternate spots along each row change from black to white along the sequence, with each row starting with the black or white circles alternately.

3 **b** The position of the right angle of the L-shape follows a repeating pattern of: bottom-right, top-left, bottom-left, top-right. So the next shape will have the corner in the top left. The square alternates between being at the end of a line on the L-shape and part way along one side, so the next shape will be part way along. The shading of the square follows the repeating pattern of: an X–black spot–black shading. So the next pattern will have a black square.

4 **e** The Z-shape faces left and right alternately; the spot alternates between black and white; the number of short lines across one arm of the Z increases by one each time.

5 **b** The halved circles alternate with quartered circles; the shading on the halved circles rotates 90° clockwise while the shading on the quartered circle rotates 90° anticlockwise.

6 **b** The number of short vertical lines follows a repeating pattern of 1–2–3–4 along the whole shape; the lower squares all have a black spot in the top left corner; the shape in the top right corner of the lower squares is the same as the shape in the top left corner of the preceding square in the upper row.

7 **b** The number of upside-down U-shapes along the top row follows the pattern of 3–2–1–2, so the next is 3. The U-shapes along the bottom row follow the pattern of 2–1–0–1, so the next is 2. The circles alternate between black and white shading.

8 **c** The end of the top horizontal line follows a repeating pattern of: plain line–X–black spot. The short horizontal lines increase from 1 to 4 then start again at 1, with the first two added to the left and the next two added to the right. The short line at the bottom of the vertical line alternates between pointing to the left and to the right.

9 **3190** $10^2 = 100$; $100 \times 0.0319 = 3.19$; $10^3 = 1000$; $3.19 \times 1000 = 3190$

10 **110** Remove the same amount of zeros from both numbers to simplify the sum: $220\,000 \div 2000 = 220 \div 2 = 110$

11 **Three hundred and fifty thousand, one hundred and two**

12 20 1<u>5</u>0<u>5.6</u>6 9<u>1</u>9<u>1</u>.<u>1</u>19 1<u>1</u> <u>3</u>67.<u>4</u>82
    $5 + 6 + 1 + 1 + 3 + 4 = 20$

13 **7998** $10\,000 − 2002 = 7998$

14 To multiply a number by 10, move it one place to the left across the decimal point. To multiply it by 1000, move it three places. To divide, move the number to the right. Move it one place to divide by 10 and two places to divide by 100.

	× 10	× 1000	÷ 10	÷ 100
3.4	34	3 400	0.34	0.034
16.78	167.8	16 780	1.678	0.1678
4750	47 500	4 750 000	475	47.50

15 a 7948.9   b 7949   c 7950   d 7900

16 **10 000, 10, 10 000**
    $100 \times 10^2 = 100 \times 100 = 10\,000$; $10\,000 \div 1000 = 10$;
    $10 \times 10^3 = 10 \times 1000 = 10\,000$

17 **240** To be divided by 5 exactly must end in 5 or 0, so that eliminates 222 and 453. To be divided exactly by 3 the digits must add up to 3, 6 or 9; 240 gives 6, so yes; 445 gives 13 which gives 4, so no; 289 gives 10, so no. Check that 240 can be divided exactly by 4; $240 \div 4 = 60$, so yes. 240 is a multiple of 3, 4 and 5.

18 **56, 700, 168** 49, 56, 700, 210, 168 can all be divided exactly by 7, but only 56, 700 and 168 can also be divided exactly by 4.

19 **−7°** Falling 13° will go below zero giving a negative number; the difference is $13 − 6 = 7$, so −7°.

20 **52** The prime numbers between 20 and 30 are 23 and 29, so total is $23 + 29 = 52$

21 **−2°** −11° up by 13° goes to 2°, a fall of 4° takes it down to −2°.

22 **125** **216** 333 525 900 **1000**
    125 is $5 \times 5 \times 5$; 216 is $6 \times 6 \times 6$;
    1000 is $10 \times 10 \times 10$

23 **2 and 21; 3 and 14; 6 and 7** $2 \times 21 = 42$; $3 \times 14 = 42$; $6 \times 7 = 42$

24 **60** 60 can be divided exactly by 2, 3, 4 and 5 so they are all factors of 60; $60 \div 2 = 30$; $60 \div 3 = 20$; $60 \div 4 = 15$; $60 \div 5 = 12$

Learning Paper 2: Logic and Shapes

1 **b** All except b have three small circles and a triangle in addition to the larger circle.

2 **a** All except a have the small striped square in the middle of the longer side. You could also accept option d as it is the only one with all 3 inner shapes aligned vertically or because the 5 dots are on the part protruding out of the square part of the outer shape.

3 **e** All except e have the wavy arrow line starting and ending outside the enclosed shape.

4 **c** All except c have five lines or elements.

5 **e** All of the shapes on the left are triangles, and the white triangles have a dotted line inside the triangle and the shaded triangles have a dotted line on the outside.

6 **d** All the shapes are made up of a wavy line which has one loop and an arrowhead at one end. Between the loop and the arrowhead there is a black circle.

7 **e** All of the shapes on the left are made up of two squares which overlap at one corner and have the overlapping section shaded.

8 **d** All of the shapes on the left have a wavy line that extends across a circle, with a black circle and a small X on the line but not at the end of the line.

9 **d** All of the shapes on the left are circular coils starting with a black spot in the middle and with a black arrowhead; they coil in an anticlockwise direction.

10 **b** All of the triangles on the left have a shaded circle on the outside of one corner of the triangle, a white circle inside the triangle and a circle overlapping one line with the inner segment shaded black.

11 **e** All of the shapes on the left are made up of four straight lines with two intersections (points where lines cross over each other).

12 **d** All of the shapes on the left have a single plain, straight arrow crossing over them.

13 **90 m** 3000 books ÷ 10 books per shelf = 300 shelves needed; 300 × 30 cm = 9000 cm; 100 cm = 1 m so 9000 cm = 90 m

14 **£22** 20 ÷ 5 = 4 so the total ticket cost for the class is £40 × 4 = £160; total cost with bus is £160 + £280 = £440; total cost shared between 20 children is £440 ÷ 20 = £22

15 Begin by placing the largest and smallest numbers at each end of a row or column. For example, place 9 and 1 in the first row; 9 + 1 = 10 and 15 − 10 = 5, so this must be the middle number in that row. Continue adding larger numbers in the opposite corners to smaller numbers and deducting their total from 15 to find the numbers between them. Example:

9	5	1
4	3	8
2	7	6

16 **45** Multiples of 5 between 20 and 66 which are odd numbers are 25, 35, 45, 55, 65, and the only one of these which is a multiple of 3 is 45.

17 **16** As Ben is a third of his mother's age, her age must be a multiple of 3; his dad is 4 times the age of Ben's sister, so his age must be a multiple of 4; his father is 4 years older than his mother, so find multiples of 3 and 4 that have a difference of 4 (12 and 16, 24 and 28, 36 and 40 and 48 and 52 all have a difference of 4). There is a difference of 3 yrs between Ben and his sister, so divide the pairs of multiples by 3 and 4 to find which have a difference of 3: 48 ÷ 3 = 16; 52 ÷ 4 = 13; 16 − 13 = 3.
Algebra can also be used to solve the problem:
If B represents Ben's age, then B = Sister + 3, and Sister = B − 3; also B = Mother ÷ 3, so Mother = 3B. But as Father = Sister × 4 and Father also = Mother + 4, it follows that Sister × 4 = Mother + 4
Then substitute B − 3 for Sister and 3B for Mother gives (B − 3) × 4 = 3B + 4
4B − 12 = 3B + 4; subtract 3B from both sides
B − 12 = 4 add 12 to both sides
B = 16

18 **6** House numbers from the main road:
2 4 6 8 10 ~~12 14~~ 16 18 20 22 24 26 28 with the 6th and 7th taken down, then count back 8 houses from number 26: 24, 22, 20, 18, 16, 10, 8, **6**

19 a **14 km** G to F to A which is 4 + 10 = 14 km
b **27 km** D to C to B to F to E is 11 + 4 + 3 + 9 = 27 km
c **B and C** or **E and F**

20 **50** 15 yellow, which is 3× as many as green, so 5 green; blue is 20 more than green, so 5 + 20 = 25 blue; twice as many red as blue, so red is 25 × 2 = 50

21 **7 weeks 1 day** 1 litre leaks every 8 hours so, as 3 × 8 = 24 hours this is 3 litres a day; half the tank is 150 litres, so 150 ÷ 3 days = 50 days which is 7 weeks and 1 day.

22 **23** Find a number that is a multiple of 3 and 4 to find his uncle's age (12, 24, 36, 48, 60, and so on); as Taz is 5 yrs older than his brother and 1 yr less than his cousin, add these to find the difference between their ages needs to be 6; 72 ÷ 3 = 24 and 72 ÷ 4 = 18; 24 − 18 = 6 years difference; subtract 1 from the age of his cousin to find Taz is 23. It could also be worked out by: 3 × cousin = 4 × brother; cousin = (T + 1) brother = (T − 5), so 3 (T + 1) = 4 (T − 5)
Multiply out the brackets gives 3T + 3 = 4T − 20, subtract 3T from both sides, 3 = T − 20 and T = 3 + 20 = 23

Learning Paper 3: Number Skills and Grids

1 **155** Work out the equation above the line first: $\frac{1}{2} \times 620 = 310$; 310 ÷ 2 = 155

2 **$2\frac{3}{4}$** The difference between $5\frac{1}{2}$ and $2\frac{3}{4}$ is $2\frac{3}{4}$

3 **24** 12 orange, which is one-tenth, so 120 flags; half are blue, so 60 blue; orange and blue make up 72 flags, and of the remaining 48 half are red and half are green, so 24 are red.

4 **9** His mother's age can be divided exactly by 4 and 3 as Nathan is $\frac{1}{4}$ of her age and his sister is $\frac{1}{3}$ of her age. As he is 3 yrs younger than his sister, find multiples of 3 and 4 that have a difference of 3; 36 ÷ 4 = 9 and 36 ÷ 3 = 12; 12 − 9 = 3

5 **£1000** Work backwards through the calculation:
$\frac{1}{4} \times £24\,000 = £6000$; $\frac{1}{3} \times £6000 = £2000$;
$\frac{1}{2} \times £2000 = £1000$ OR: $\frac{1}{2} \times \frac{1}{3} \times \frac{1}{4} \times 24\,000 = \frac{24\,000}{24} = 1000$

6 **28** $\frac{7}{8} \times 16 = 14$; 14 × 2 = 28

7 **2** 10 350.4 × 10 = 103 504; 103 504 × 2 = 207 008; so 207 008 ÷ 2 = 103 504

8 **£105** Area of floor is 2.5 × 3.5 sq metres = 8.75 sq metres; £12 × 8.75 = £105. Multiply 2.5 by 3.5 to find the total area; remove the decimal points from both numbers and multiply as normal (25 × 35 = 875); count the number of digits after the decimal in the original sum to find how many digits are after the decimal in the answer (there is a total of 2 digits after the decimals in 2.5 × 3.5, so the answer is 8.75); 12 × 8.75 = 105

9 a **£42** A starter and dessert costs £5.25 × 2 = £10.50; starter and dessert for 4 is £10.50 × 4 = £42

   b **£4.10** Set menu for 2 is £17.95 × 2 = £35.90, change from £40 is £40 − £35.90 = £4.10

   c **£1.05** Starter and dessert for £10.50 plus cheapest main at £8.50 = £19, so the saving is £19 − £17.95 = £1.05

10 **1 010 305** Multiplying by 1000 the decimal point moves three places to the right as the number gets bigger.

11 **0.1** $10^3 = 1000$, so the decimal point moves three places to the right.

12 a **16** 2 break, 98 are shared into boxes of 6, which gives 16 half dozen boxes and 2 left over.

   b **2**

   c **£16.80** 16 half dozen boxes gives 8 dozen eggs; 8 × £2.10 = £16.80

13 **19%** 42 + 17 + 22 = 81; 100 − 81 = 19 green sweets, 19 out of 100 is 19%

14 **£4250** 10% is £1275 ÷ 3 = £425, so 100% is £425 × 10 = £4250

15 **150** 20% of 500 = 100, 40% is 200 and 60% is 300. Add these together to find 600. Half of the school is 250 so 250 pupils learn two languages and 250 × 2 languages = 500; 600 − 500 = 100 pupils who learn 1 language. Subtract this from the remaining 250 pupils to find 150 pupils who do not learn any languages (250 − 100 = 150).

16 **£150** 90% of original cost of bag is £54 so the full price is $\frac{54}{9} \times 10 = £60$; 90% of original cost of dress is £81 so the full price is $\frac{81}{9} \times 10 = £90$. The total of the two items at original price is £60 + £90 = £150

17 **c** The missing square has an uphill diagonal arrow from bottom left to top right and the same small shape as in the corner of the adjacent outer rectangle.

18 **e** Of the two shapes in every square, the shape on the left side of the square is the same down each column and the same relative position within the square. The shape on the right side is the same across each row and in the same relative position in each square across the row.

19 **d** The outer white shape in each of the outer squares is repeated in the inner position of the next square moving anticlockwise round the grid; it is adjacent to the central square and has the same shading as the quarter of the central square next to it. The inner shape in each outer square moves clockwise into the outer position of the adjacent square.

20 **e** The middle row follows a pattern of circles and squares alternating. The shading of the triangles and circles is the same diagonally across the grid, from top left to bottom right. The thick horizontal lines and the thick vertical lines are next to one another in the middle of top and bottom row.

21 **b** The outer black shapes in the squares on the right are a reflection of the black shapes in the squares on the left-hand side; the small circle has the same shading and relative position down the columns.

22 **c** The missing triangle is a reflection of the outer triangle at the top of the shape.

Learning Paper 4: Transformations, Ratios and Proportions

1 d
2 b
3 e
4 e
5 c
6 e
7 d
8 c
9 c
10 d

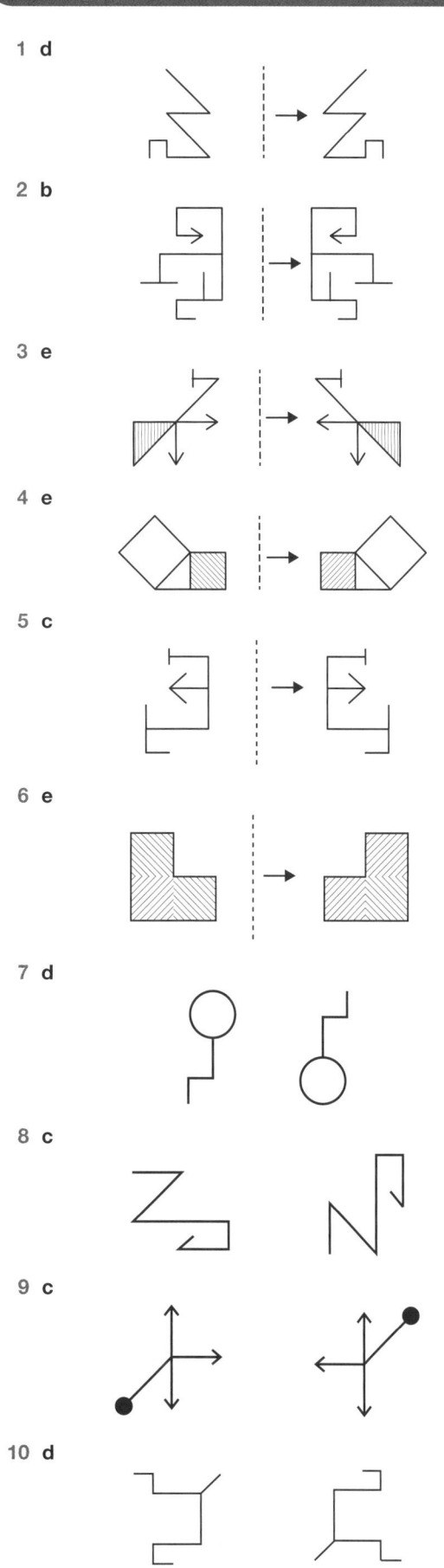

11 a **225 g sugar** 150 g is 2 portions of the ratio for 15 biscuits, so one portion is 75 g, and sugar is one portion, so 45 biscuits need 75 g × 3 = 225 g sugar
    b **450 g butter** 150 g butter for 15 biscuits, so 150 g × 3 = 450 g butter for 45 biscuits.
    c **675 g flour** One portion is 75 g, flour has 3 portions, with 3 × 75 g of flour for 15 biscuits. So for 45 biscuits the flour needed is 3 × 75 g × 3 = 675 g
12 **1600 ml or 1.6 litres** The amount of juice is $\frac{1}{3}$ × 12 litres = 4 litres; the amount of diluted squash is $\frac{2}{3}$ × 12 litres = 8 litres; of the 8 litres of diluted squash, $\frac{1}{5}$ is concentrate and $\frac{4}{5}$ is water. $\frac{1}{5}$ × 8 litres = 1.6 litres, which is equivalent to 1600 ml.
13 The recipe is for 25 cakes, so for 35 cakes divide each amount by 5 and multiply by 7 (as the ratio of 25 : 35 simplifies to 5 : 7).
    a **490 g flour** 350 g ÷ 5 = 70 g, 70 g × 7 = 490 g
    b **350 g butter** 250 g ÷ 5 = 50 g, 50 g × 7 = 350 g
    c **210 g sugar** 150 g ÷ 5 = 30 g, 30 g × 7 = 210 g
14 **£4000** If 15% is £600, the 5% is 600 ÷ 3 = £200, and the full amount is £200 × 20 = £4000
15 **£12.07** The number of litres required is 102 km ÷ 12 = 8.5 litres; the cost is £1.42 × 8.5 = £12.07
16 **£6** If 5 apples cost £2.50, each apple is 50p. 12 × 50p = £6. One-quarter is 543 ÷ 3 = 181, so the whole number is 181 × 4 = 724
17 **30 m per minute** 50 cm per second is 0.5 m per second, so per minute is 0.5 × 60 = 30 metres per minute
18 **770 g** 220 g ÷ 2 = 110 g for one portion; the flour required is 7 portions, so 110 g × 7 = 770 g
19 **£9.10** 56 km ÷ 8 = 7; 7 × £1.30 = £9.10

Learning Paper 5: Algebra and Codes

1 $\frac{7}{8}$ ($\frac{1}{2}$ × $\frac{3}{4}$) + $\frac{1}{2}$ = $\frac{3}{8}$ + $\frac{1}{2}$ = $\frac{3}{8}$ + $\frac{4}{8}$ = $\frac{7}{8}$
2 **87** $\frac{3}{5}$ × (120 + 25) = $\frac{3}{5}$ × 145 = 3 × 29 = 87
3 **500** ($\frac{3}{4}$ × 640) + 20 = (3 × 160) + 20 = 480 + 20 = 500
4 **63** ($\frac{30}{4}$ − $\frac{1}{2}$) × (0.3 × 30) = ($\frac{30}{4}$ − $\frac{2}{4}$) × 9 = $\frac{28}{4}$ × 9 = 7 × 9 = 63
5 **194** ($\frac{1}{2}$ × 364) + ($\frac{1}{4}$ × 48) = 182 + 12 = 194
6 **63** x^2 is 5 × 5 = 25; 7x is 7 × 5 = 35; 25 + 35 + 3 = 63
7 **19** Work out the equation in the brackets first; 5a is 5 × 7 = 35 and 35 + 3 = 38; then divide by 2; 38 ÷ 2 = 19
8 **31** 3x − 21 = 72, so 3x = 72 + 21 = 93, and x = 93 ÷ 3 = 31
9 **80** $\frac{1}{2}x$ + 14 = 54, so $\frac{1}{2}x$ = 54 − 14 = 40, and x = 40 × 2 = 80
10 a **19** Substituting gives: 2 × 7 + 8 − 3 = 14 + 8 − 3 = 19
    b **27** Substituting gives: 3 × 8 − 7 + 10 = 24 − 7 + 10 = 27
    c **36** Substituting gives: $\frac{(3 \times 8)}{3}$ + 4 × 7 = 8 + 28 = 36
11 **7** 10x − 49 = 3x, subtract 3x from each side of the equation 7x − 49 = 0, so 7x = 49 and x = 7
12 **70** Substituting gives (2 × 11) + (2 × 5 × 5) − ($\frac{1}{2}$ × 4) = 22 + 50 − 2 = 70
13 **12** Work out the brackets first: 3a is 3 × 5 = 15 and 3b is 3 × 11 = 33; 15 + 33 = 48; c = 4 so divide by 4; 48 ÷ 4 = 12
14 **6** 3x + 12 = 5x, subtract 3x from each side of the equation gives 12 = 2x, so x = 6
15 **4** 21x − 4 = 5x + 60, subtract 5x from each side of the equation sign to get 16x − 4 = 60; therefore 16x = 64 as 64 − 4 = 60; 64 ÷ 16 = 4, so x = 4
16 **e** The first letter represents the position of the two short lines across the U-shape (D is at one end, E is in the middle, F is part way along one side); the second letter represents the circle style (X is a double white circle, Y has a central black circle, Z is a single white circle).
17 **b** The first letter represents the line pattern on the end-facing square (A is an L-shape, B is a U-shape, C is a square); the second letter represents the orientation of the cube (P shows the lower and left side face, Q shows the top right face, R shows the top left face). As the shape given shows the lower right face it will have a new letter code, hence S in the given options.
18 **c** The first letter represents the shading of the circle (A has a cross, B is black, C has lined shading); the second letter represents the orientation of the rectangle (M is horizontal, N is vertical); the third letter represents that second shape within the rectangle (X is a white square, Y is a triangle, Z is a cross-hatched square).
19 **e** The first letter represents the style of the arrowhead on the top horizontal line (A is a simple V-shape, B is a white triangle, C is a black triangle); the second letter represents the line style of the diagonal arrow (G is dashed, H is plain); the third letter represents the line style of the top horizontal arrow (R is a plain line, S is a double line, T is a single dashed line).
20 **b** The first letter represents the number of points where the curved line crosses straight lines (A is 2, B is 3, C is 4); the second letter represents the lengths of the lines of the L-shapes (E has varying lengths, F has all three Ls with equal length lines); the third letter represents the coloured spots (X has one black and one white, Y has two black, Z has two white).
21 **e** The first letter represents the number of black spots (M is 2, N is 1); the second letter is the shading style of the circle (X is white, Y has diagonal lines, Z has a cross); the third letter represents the position of the triangle along the top of the rectangle (A is at the left with the right angle in the middle, B is at the right with the right angle at the end, C is at the left with the right angle at the end, D is at the right with the right angle in the middle).
22 **c** The first letter represents the shape at the end of the line pattern (A is a black circle, B is a white circle, C is a small black triangle); the second letter represents the number of straight lines in the line pattern (L is 3, M is 4); the third letter represents the angles between the lines (Y has all right angles, Z has angles of different sizes).

23 **a** The first letter represents the position of the shaded circle inside the square (A is top left, B is bottom left, D is top right, so the bottom right will be a different letter – hence C in the answer options); the second letter represents the number of black triangles (X is 2, Y is 1).

24 **e** The first letter represents the number of sides on the shape (A is 6, B is 5, C is 4); the second letter represents the shading style of the circle (X is white, Y has a cross, Z is black).

25 **d** The first letter represents the style of the horizontal line across the top of the shape (L is straight, M is zig-zag, N is curved joining U-shapes); the second letter represents the pattern of the left side of the shape (P is diagonal line shading, Q has a black circle, R has a white heart shape).

26 **a** The first letter represents the number of black spots (A is 1, B is 3, C is 2); the second letter represents the total number of spots in the rectangle (X is 3, Y is 5, Z is 7).

27 **c** The first letter represents the 'leaf' number and location on the flower shape (D has 1, E has 2 at the base, F has 2 part-way up); the second letter represents the shading of the central circle (A has diagonal lines, B has crossed lines and C has spots); the third letter represents the number of curves ('petals') around the top circle (A has 7, B has 6, C has 5).

28 **c** The first letter represents the number of black circles (A is 2, B is 3, C is 4); the second letter represents the number of white circles (D is 2, E is 3, F is 4); the third letter represents the outer shape (G is a heart, H is a comma-shape facing left, J is a comma-shape facing right).

29 **d** The first letter represents the shading of the shape inside the square (A is black, B is white, C is diagonal lines); the second letter represents the shape inside the square (X is a circle, Z is a triangle, so another letter must represent the square – Y is given in the answer options).

30 **b** The first letter represents the orientation of the 'fish' shape (L is facing right, M is facing down, N is facing up, so another letter must represent facing left – O is given in the answer options); the second letter represents the 'eye' (Y is a black spot, X is no 'eye', Z is a white circle).

Learning Paper 6: Measurement

1 **620.4 g** 0.5 kg + 120 g + 400 mg = 500 g + 120 g + 0.4 g = 620.4 g

2 **300 000 mm** 0.3 km = 300 m, 1 m = 1000 mm, so 300 m = 300 000 mm

3 **150 000 cm** 1.5 km = 1,500 m, 1 m = 100 cm, so 1500 m = 150 000 cm

4 **750 000 mm** 0.75 km = 750 m, 1 m = 1000 mm, so 750 m = 750 000 mm

5 **3440 ml** 4.2 litres – 760 ml = 4200 ml – 760 ml = 3440 ml

6 **433 m** 170 m + 300 cm + 0.26 km = 170 m + 3 m + 260 m = 433 m

7 **3.7 kg** The difference between 6.35 kg and 10.05 kg is 10.05 kg – 6.35 kg = 3.7 kg

8 **49.8 cm** 46 mm, 3.2 cm and 0.42 m = 4.6 cm = 3.2 cm + 42 cm = 49.8 cm

9 **3 400 000 mm** 3.4 km = 3400 m = 3 400 000 mm

10 **£5250** Volume of the container is 20 × 5 × 3 cubic metres = 300 cubic metres; the cost for one week is £35 × 300 ÷ 4 = £2625, so the cost for 2 weeks is £2625 × 2 = £5250

11 **10 litres** Each wall is 6 m × 2 m = 12 m²; 4 walls are 48 m², 2 coats of emulsion is 48 × 2 = 96 m²; $2\frac{1}{2}$ litres covers 24 m² so divide 96 by 24 to find how many lots of $2\frac{1}{2}$ are needed (96 ÷ 24 = 4) and multiply this by $2\frac{1}{2}$ to find the amount of litres ($4 \times 2\frac{1}{2} = 10$)

12 **24.5 cm** A heptagon has 7 sides, so 7 × 3.5 = 24.5 cm

13 **1 litre** Volume of the 10 cm cube is 10 cm × 10 cm × 10 cm = 1000 cm³; 1 cm³ holds 1 ml, so 1000 cm³ holds 1000 ml = 1 litre

14 **8** The perimeter is 430 m + 310 m + 360 m + 400 m = 1500 m; 12 km = 12 000 m; remove the same amount of zeros from both numbers to divide; 120 ÷ 15 = 8 so 12 000 ÷ 1500 = 8

15 **13 cm** The total of both widths is 3 cm × 2 = 6 cm; subtract this from 32 to find the total of both lengths (32 – 6 = 26) then divide by 2 to find one length (26 ÷ 2 = 13)

16 **a 48** A cube has 12 edges and along each edge 4 cubes will have 2 faces painted (the corners are not included as they will have 3 faces painted); 12 × 4 = 48

   b 8 cubes at the corners giving the vertices of the larger cube will have three faces painted red, and the large cube has 8 vertices.

   c 64 Cubes with no red faces form the inner cube which is made up of 4 × 4 × 4 cubes = 64 cubes

17 **11.00 a.m.** Half of the 16 km walk is 8 km, at 4 km per hour will take 2 hours, 9 a.m. plus 2 hours is 11 a.m.

18 **73 minutes** or **1 hour and 13 minutes** Travelling at 60 km per hour is 1 km per minute, so 48 km takes 48 minutes. The journey includes a 25-minute break, so the total journey time is 48 + 25 minutes = 73 minutes, which is 1h 13 minutes.

19 **a 100** 200 gallons in the morning so 400 gallons per day. Each cow gives 4 gallons, so the number of cows is 400 ÷ 4 = 100

   b 42 gallons The average per cow is 4 gallons per day. Daisy gives 150% of 4 = 6 gallons per day, so in a week she gives 6 × 7 = 42 gallons

20 **a 40 km** From Bidden to Carbury by train takes 15:07 – 14:37 = 30 mins; travelling at 80 km per hour will cover 40 km in half an hour, so the distance is 40 km.

   b 1 hour (or **60 minutes**) The journey by road is 40 km + 10 km = 50 km, so a car travelling at 50 km per hour takes 1 hour.

21 **$1\frac{1}{2}$ hours** (or **90 minutes**) Half of the journey is 60 km and it takes 1 hour; the second half takes half the amount of time, that is $\frac{1}{2}$ hour, so the total journey time is $1\frac{1}{2}$ hours.

22 **a 20:55** At midnight the tide had been coming in for 06:17 – 03:12 = 3 hours 5 minutes; so low tide was 3 hours 5 minutes before midnight, which is 24:00 – 03:05 = 20:55

   b 09:29 6 hours 17 minutes later than 03:12 is 09:29.

Learning Paper 7: Geometry and Nets

1. Angles in a triangle add up to 180°.
   a. **70°** 180 − (75 + 35) = 180 − 110 = 70
   b. **36°** 180 − (94 + 50) = 180 − 144 = 36
   c. **35°** 180 − (86 + 59) = 180 − 145 = 35
2. a. **156°, because angles on a straight line add up to 180°.** $x + 24 = 180$ on the line that is at an angle; 180 − 24 = 156
   b. **72°, because vertically opposite angles equal 180°** or **angles on a straight line add up to 180°**, or **the sum of the angles in a triangle is 180°**.
3. a. **45°, because the base angles of right angled isosceles triangles are 45°, and the total of a right angle is 90°**
   b. **30°, because the angles of an equilateral triangle are 60°, and the total of a right angle is 90°**
4. a. **NW** From N 135° clockwise takes Sam to SE, 180° from SE is NW.
   b. **135 degrees clockwise** or **225 degrees anticlockwise**
5–6 When reflected in the y axis, the points will be on the opposite side of the vertical line. When reflected in the x axis, this points will be on the opposite side of the horizontal line. The points will be the same distance from the lines each time.
5. A' (−2,5)
   B' (−1,1)
   C' (−4,2)
6. Always read the value off the x axis first.
   a. (3,−2)
   b. (3,4)
   c. (−3,−4)
7. **c** The circle cannot be adjacent to an edge which has a straight side of the right-angled triangle.
8. **a** The base of the U-shape cannot be along an edge adjacent to a face with an X.
9. **b** A face with a U-shape cannot have the edge along the base of its 'U' next to the base of a 'U' on an adjacent face.
10. **e** The face with the black arrow cannot have the arrow perpendicular to the lines of the face with straight-line shading.
11. **b** All except cube b can be made as the face with two black spots cannot be adjacent to the face with one black spot.
12. **d** Cube d is the only one that can be made; in cube a the triangle cannot be adjacent to the U-shape; in b the base of the U-shape cannot be adjacent to the circle; cube c does not have two faces with U-shapes; in e the white arrow cannot point to face the circle.
13. **e** Cube e is the only one that can be made; in cube a the arrow does not point to the face with the P-shape; in b the base of the U-shape cannot be adjacent to the top of the @ shape; in c the open side of the U-shape cannot be adjacent to the @ shape; in d the base of the arrow cannot come out of the left-hand side of the @ shape.
14. **c** C is the only one that can be made; in cube a there is no black triangle in the net; in b the base of the U-shape cannot be adjacent to the arrow; in d the arrow cannot point away from the white circle; in e the arrow cannot be adjacent to the cross.

Learning Paper 8: Statistics

1. a. **46** Take numbers for each fruit from the graph: 9 + 7 + 8 + 12 + 10 = 46
   b. **grapes and bananas** 20% is the same as $\frac{1}{5}$ and $\frac{1}{5}$ of 46 is 9.2. There cannot be part of a child, therefore which fruits were chosen by ten or more children? Grapes (10) and bananas (12).
   c. **6** $\frac{1}{3} \times 12 = 4$; the new total for apples is 9 + 4 = 13; the difference between apples and oranges is 13 − 7 = 6
2. a. **78%** (accept 79%)
   b. **48 marks** 50 marks × 2 = 100% so divide by 2 (96% ÷ 2 = 48)
   c. **Pupil C** If 50 marks is 100% then 31 marks is 62%.
   d. **58%** H has 66%, I has 50%, J has 58%; the average is 66 + 50 + 58 = 174 and 174 ÷ 3 = 58
3. a. **1 hour 45 mins** 9 a.m. to 11 a.m. is 2 hours, minus 15 minutes break gives 1 hour 45 mins.
   b. **1.45 p.m.**
   c. **1 hour 30 mins** 11 a.m. to 12.30 p.m. is $1\frac{1}{2}$ hours or 1 hour 30 mins.
   d. **14 km** 10 km + 4 km = 14 km
4. a. **8 days**
   b. **0.7 cm per day** 0–7 cm in 10 days, so the average over the first 10 days is $\frac{7}{10} = 0.7$ cm per day.
   c. **7th** The slowest rate of growth shows on the graph as the least steep line, which is on the 7th day.
   d. **days 1–4** It grows 4 cm in the first 4 days, giving an average of 1 cm per day.
5. a. **119 cm** Range is the highest value less the lowest value, 213 − 94 = 119 cm
   b. **39 cm** The difference is 207 cm − 168 cm = 39 cm
6. a. **28 km**
   b. **5 km** Sandon to Towie is 40 km, Sandon to Umber is 45 km, the difference is 5 km. Look at where the row and column for Radford and Vacton meet.
   c. **1 hour 10 mins** (or **70 mins**) Towie to Vacton is 70 km, travelling at 60 km per hour is 1 km per minute, so it takes 70 mins which is 1 hour 10 minutes.
7. a. **90, 90, 95** 12 + 15 + 14 + 16 + 15 + 18 = 90; 10 + 12 + 13 + 17 + 18 + 20 = 90; 14 + 16 + 16 + 17 + 13 + 19 = 95
   b. **15** Average is the total divided by the number of rounds, 90 ÷ 6 = 15
   c. **Harry** Range is the highest minus the lowest. Ginny 18−12 = 6; Harry 20−10 = 10; Indigo 19−13 = 6; the widest range is Harry's: 10.
   d. **57** Round 6 had each person's highest score, the total was 18 + 20 + 19 = 57
8. a. **C** and **D** Totals: A has 3 + 4 + 2 + 4=13; B has 3 + 5 + 4 + 2 + 3=17; C has 3 + 1 + 2 + 4 =10; D has 2 + 3 + 2 + 1 + 3 = 11; E has 4 + 5 + 2 + 3 + 1 = 15; so C and D do not qualify.
   b. **3** Average is the total divided by 5, so for team E 15 ÷ 5 = 3
   c. **17** *see part a*

9 a **10** Team A 2 + 1 + 5 + 2 = 10
   b **10 matches.** As the scores for each team are shown on the left along each row, each match is shown twice. Count the number of scores shown then divide by 2: 20 ÷ 2 = 10
   c **0** Team D's scores were 4–5, 3–4, 1–3, 1–3 so no wins.
   d **2** 3 + 0 + 3 + 2 = 8 and 8 ÷ 4 = 2
   e **Team B** Their scores were 4–2, 1–0, 4–3, 5–3 showing 4 wins.
   f A has **2**, B has **8**, C has **5**, D has **0**, E has **5**
10 **45** The number of hours is the distance divided by speed, 540 ÷ 60 = 9 hours per day, 9 × 5 = 45 hours in a week.
11 a **3** Feb, Nov and Dec are all greater than 35 mm.
   b **18 mm** The average is $\frac{(18 + 16 + 22 + 16)}{4} = \frac{72}{4} = 18$ mm
   c **22 mm** The highest is 38 mm, the lowest is 16 mm, the range is the difference 38 − 16 = 22
12 **54 minutes** Travelling at 20 km per hour it will take $1\frac{1}{2}$ hours or 90 mins to do 30 km; divide 50 km per 60 mins by 5 to find 10 km per 12 mins (50 ÷ 5 = 10 and 60 ÷ 5 = 12) then multiply by 3 to find 30 km per 36 mins (10 × 3 = 30 and 12 × 3 = 36); the difference in time taken is 90 − 36 = 54 minutes.
13 a **1** 5% of 20 = 1 (20 × 5 = 100 and 100 ÷ 100 = 1)
   b **75** 15% of 500 = 75 (500 × 15 = 7500 and 7500 ÷ 100 = 75)
   c **Pasta and fishcakes** (51%) OR **pasta and pizza** (69%)
   d **120 degrees** $\frac{1}{3}$ of 360 degrees is 120 degrees.
   e **60 degrees** $\frac{1}{6}$ × 360 = 60 degrees

Curveball Questions 1

1 **8 hours** Area of pond is 2.5 m × 8 m = 20 m²; 50 ml evaporates from each square metre per hour in the sun, which is 50 × 20 ml per hour for the whole pond, that is 1 litre per hour. With 8 hours of sun in 1 day, 8 litres will evaporate from pond, so in a week 8 × 7 = 56 litres are lost. The hosepipe gives 7 litres per hour so it needs 8 hours to give 56 litres.

2
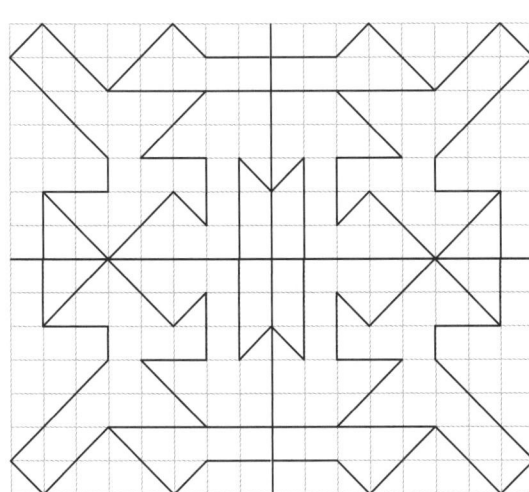

3

2	1	2	2	6
4		1		7
9	9	9		7
3	3		4	9
0		1	2	0

Mixed Paper 1

1 **e** The second shape has the rectangle rotated through 90 degrees, and the small shape in the upper right corner is repeated the number of times indicated by the number of black spots, with the same shading style as the small shape in the lower left corner of the first rectangle.
2 **d** The second pattern has one more white circle than there are black circles in the first shape, linked with a single plain line in a vertical direction.
3 **a** The second pattern has an L-shape with the two shapes from the centre of the circle separated; the larger shape from inside the circle is at the top left with the shading of the central shape, and the central shape is at the lower right and has the shading of the larger shape.
4 **e** The second pattern has the shapes from the left side of the square added to the squares on the right side; the left side squares are removed giving a vertically orientated rectangle and the shape in the top left of the square becomes shaded in the style of the square in the top right section of the first pattern.
5 **15** 5<u>4</u>73.0<u>5</u>16   108.0<u>2</u>3
   1<u>2</u>98.6<u>1</u>9 4 + 5 + 1 + 2 + 2 + 1 = 15
6 **17 072 702**
7 **Four hundred and ninety-six point six**
   1000 − 503.4 = 496.6
8 **21 890 000** 22 000 000 − 110 000 = 21 890 000
9 a **2½ kg** Read through the whole question to find the best place to start and change kg into grams (1 kg = 1000 g): A = 3000 g and B is 500 g lighter than A so it is 2500 g (3000 − 500 = 2500); B is 500 g heavier than D so D is 2000 g (2500 − 500 = 2000); C is 250 g heavier than D so it is 2250 g (2000 + 250 = 2250); and C is 500 g lighter than E so E is 2750 g (2250 + 500 = 2750). A is the heaviest and D is the lightest.
   b **A**
   c **D**
10 **420** Strawberry is 60; vanilla is 60 × 2 = 120; chocolate is 120 × 2 = 240; the total number of ice creams is 60 + 120 + 240 = 420
11 **10p** Total spend is £1.75 + 80p + £1.15 = £3.70; change from £5 is £1.30, made up of £1 coin, 20p coin and therefore a 10p coin to make the full amount.
12 a **£60** 400 × 15 = 6000 and 6000 ÷ 100 = 60
   b **£500** Value plus tax is £400 + £60 = £460; 10% of value is 400 × 10 = 4000 and 4000 ÷ 100 = 40; so the importer must sell at £460 + £40 = £500

13 **£4000** If 5% is £1000, then 10% is £2000 and 20% is £4000.
14 **£535.60** 520 × 3 = 1560 and 1560 ÷ 100 = 15.6; £520 + £15.60 = £535.60 or 1% of £520 = £5.20, so 3% = £5.20 × 3 = £15.60; the new rent is £520 + £15.60 = £535.60
15 **b** The small shape in the corner of each square in the grid rotates clockwise around square along each row; the corner shape in the top and bottom rows alternates between black and white; the small shape in the middle of each square is repeated along each row.
16 **e** The small shapes in this triangle will be the same as the large shape in the triangle beneath it; the number of crosses indicates the number of small shapes; and the background line shading has lines perpendicular to the line shading in the lower right triangle.
17 **d** The whole grid has a diagonal line of symmetry from top left to bottom right, so the missing square in the grid will have an L-shape with the right angle of the L in the top right corner of the square, and 'arms' of the L will be equal in length.
18 **e** The squares along the centre of this grid have a circle alternating between top left and lower right corner, the shading of the circle is the same as the corner triangle in the grid square immediately above or below, and the short diagonal line from the corner alternates from the bottom left and top right corner of the square.
19 **3** If $52x + 10 = 166$, $52x = 166 - 10 = 156$, $x = \frac{156}{52} = 3$
20 **a 3** Substituting gives $6x + 5 = (3 \times 11) - 10$; $6x + 5 = 33 - 10 = 23$; $6x = 18$ and $x = 3$
   b 15 Substituting gives $(6 \times 5) + 5 = 3y - 10$; $30 + 5 = 3y - 10$; $35 = 3y - 10$; $45 = 3y$, so $y = 15$
21 **a 120** Substituting gives $3ab = 3 \times 4 \times 10 = 120$
   b 12 Substituting gives $\frac{(4 \times 10)}{8} + 7 = \frac{40}{8} + 7 = 5 + 7 = 12$
   c 158 Substituting gives $(4 \times 4) + (10 \times 10) + 42 = 16 + 100 + 42 = 158$
22 **d** The first letter represents the position of the arrow in relation to the circle (A from the centre to the outside, B passing right across, C from the outside to the inside); the second letter represents the other shape (X is a triangle, Y a square, Z a circle).
23 **d** The first letter represents the orientation of the three straight lines (A is a Z-shape, B is a U-shape, C is an N-shape, D an inverted U-shape). The second letter represents the number of loops on the curly line (X is 1, Y is 2, Z is 30. The third letter represents the shading of the circle (E has a cross, F is black, G is white).
24 **b** The first letter represents the number of circles (A is 1, B is 2, C is 3). The second letter represents the total number of shapes in the line (X is 5, Y is 4). The third letter represents the number of triangles (L is none, M is 1, N is 2).

25 **e** The first letter represents the number of short lines projecting below the triangle (A is 3, B is 2, C is 1). The second letter represents the shading style of the triangle (G is horizontal lines, H is diagonal lines, J is black). The third letter represents the number of black circles in the square (Z is 3, Y is 1, X is none).
26 **East** 45° anticlockwise from N is NW; 90° clockwise from NW is NE; 45° clockwise from NE is E.
27 **1.20 p.m.** (or **13:20**) Left at 9.30 a.m. first turn after one hour is at 10.30 a.m.; next turn after 30 minutes is at 11.00 a.m.; then two hours before the next turn is 1.00 p.m., and a final 20 minutes means arrival at the destination is at 1.20 p.m. (13:20).
28 **South-east** From south right 30° followed by left 120° faces the east, then left 45° is to the north-east, left 90° is to the north-west, and then right 180° is towards the south-east.
29 **Octagon** By turning through all eight points of the compass the shape drawn will have eight sides and be an octagon.
30 **a 52** Each division along the x axis represents two students.
   b 11 33 − 22 = 11
   c 200 22 + 33 + 52 + 41 + 29 + 23 = 200
   d 2 The first multiple of 7 after 33 is 35, so 2 more players are needed.

Mixed Paper 2

1 **d** The square in the corner of the L shape is rotated 180° and the other two squares are removed.
2 **e** The shading of the sections in the rectangle follow the order of shadings round the circle, starting with black.
3 **d** The first shape is rotated through 180 degrees to give the second shape.
4 **c** The second shape is a larger version of the first shape with a small white circle inside and the same number of small black circles on the U-loops sitting on the outside of the line where the large white circle was in the first shape.
5 **e** The second shape has the same shading as the triangle below the rectangle in the first shape, with the shape in the middle square below the second shape repeated the same number of times as there are crosses in the third square.
6 **31, 37, 41, 43, 47**
7 **a 3** 27 = 3 × 9; 39 = 3 × 13
   b 7 28 = 4 × 7; 49 = 7 × 7
8 **105** 3 × 5 × 7 = 105
9 **271** $10^3 = 10 \times 10 \times 10 = 1000$; $9^3 = 9 \times 9 \times 9 = 729$; 1000 − 729 = 271
10 **150** $\frac{3}{4} \times 300 = 75 \times 3 = 225$; $\frac{2}{3} \times 225 = 75 \times 2 = 150$
11 **1.4** $\frac{7}{8} \times \frac{4}{5} = \frac{28}{40} = \frac{14}{20} = \frac{7}{10}$; To divide fractions, invert the second fraction then multiply them; $\frac{7}{10} \div \frac{1}{2} = \frac{7}{10} \times \frac{2}{1} = \frac{14}{10} = 1\frac{4}{10} = 1.4$
12 **a £240** $\frac{3}{25} \times £2000$ so $\frac{1}{25}$ is 2000 ÷ 25 = £80, 3 × £80 = £240

b **£352** The remainder is £2000 − £240 = £1760, $\frac{4}{5}$ of that was given to a friend, so $\frac{1}{5}$ × £1760 left = £352

13 **1892.2** 4730.5 ÷ 2.5 = 47305 ÷ 25 = 1892.2
14 **134.401** 104.35 + 29.731 + 0.32 = 134.401
15 **191.04** 250.5 − 59.46 = 191.04
16 **51.78** Count the number of decimal places in the two numbers to be multiplied: 0.15 × 345.2 Here there are three. Then carry out the multiplication as a long multiplication: 15 × 3452 = 51780; then count in three from the right to find the final position for the decimal point: 5 1 7 8 0 which gives 51.780.
                                                         3 2 1

17 **e**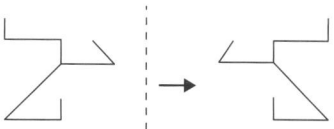

18 **b**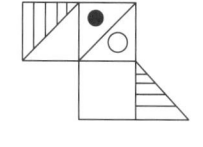

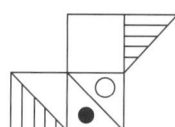

19 **d**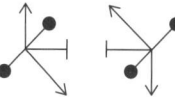

20 **c**

21 **53** 6^2 = 36 and 36 + 11 = 47; 7 × 3 = 21 so the equation can be simplified to: 47 + 21 − 15 = 53
22 **19** 2^2 = 4 and 3^3 = 27 so the equation in brackets simplifies to 7 + 4 + 27 = 38; $\frac{1}{2}$ × 38 = 19
23 **71** 450 ÷ 5 = 90; 4^2 = 16 and 16 + 3 = 19; 90 − 19 = 71
24 **12** 5^3 = 125 and 4^3 = 64; 125 − 64 − 1 = 60; 3^2 = 9 and 2^2 = 4; 9 − 4 = 5 and 60 ÷ 5 = 12
25 **128 mm** 0.02 m = 20 mm, 7.3 cm = 73 mm, so 20 + 73 + 35 = 128 mm
26 **25** 5 litres = 5000 ml, 5000 ÷ 200 = 25
27 **2782 mm** 2 m = 2000 mm, 73 cm = 730 mm, so 2000 + 730 + 52 = 2782 mm
28 **1 010 305** Multiplying by 1000 moves the digits three places to the left, increasing the number.
29 **480 cm cubes (cm³)** With all lengths in cm, 16 × 3 × 10 = 48 × 10 = 480, the volume is 480 cm cubes.
30 **144 cm** A decagon has 10 sides, so 144 mm × 10 = 1440 mm = 144 cm
31 **66** 1 sq m has 4 50 cm squares, the area of the rectangle is 3 × 5.5 sq m = 16.5 sq m, 16.5 × 4 = 66

32 a **x = 72** Angles on a straight line add up to 180 degrees and base angles of an isosceles triangle are equal.
  b **y = 36** Angles in a triangle add up to 180 degrees.
33 a **parallelogram**
  b **heptagon**
34 **46** The top score is 29 + 17 = 46; 46 − 42 = 4
35 **4** $\frac{1}{3}$ of the 12 matches scored 4 goals, giving 4 × 4 = 16 goals; $\frac{1}{4}$ of the 12 matches scored 8 goals, giving 3 × 8 = 24 goals. Then there was 1 match with 6 goals, and 1 match with 2 goals, and 3 matches with no goals. The total goals across the 12 matches is 16 + 24 + 6 + 2 + 0 + 0 + 0 = 48; 48 divided by 12 = 4
36 a **48 km per hour** 45 + 50 + 58 + 48 + 35 + 51 + 49 + 50 + 45 + 49 = 480, 480 ÷ 10 = 48
  b **23 km per hour** 58 − 35 = 23

Mixed Paper 3

1 **0, 8** The number is 500 7_0_2 033.8_9_4
2 **2 002 000.2** 100 100.01 × 20 = 2 002 000.2
3 a **9** 357.3_6_ 3 + 6 = 9
  b **12** _5_63.2_7_ 5 + 7 = 12
4 **78 030** 78.03 × 1000 = 78 030
5 **e** All of the shapes on the left have one half shaded.
6 **b** All of the shapes on the left are made up of a triangle, a circle and one short straight line.
7 **e** All of the shapes except e have the two V-shape lines crossing over to give four intersections.
8 **c** All of the shapes except c have the two short lines that project into the square projecting from opposite sides of the square.
9 **10 years** Pat is 7 years old, Kaz is 2 years younger so Kaz is 5 years, and Tom is 5 years older than Kaz, so Tom is 10 years old.
10 **Yellow** Red are blue + 23 seconds; green are blue + 12 seconds, so green are 11 seconds faster than red, and green are 10 seconds faster than yellow. So blue is the fastest, then green, then yellow and then red, so the yellow team are third.
11 **Numbers 5 and 11** The house numbers are 1 3 _5_ 7 9 _11_ 13 15 17 19, so the third is 5 and the sixth is 11.
12 **3.20 p.m.** The fish arrives 1.30 p.m. + 20 mins preparation = 1.50 p.m., then $1\frac{1}{2}$ hours with the monkeys takes the time to 3.20 p.m.
13 a **£6** £33 + £21 = £54; £54 is 90% so 100% (full price) is 54 divided by 9 × 100 = £60; so she saved £6.
  b **£27** 90% of £30 is $\frac{9}{10}$ × £30 = 9 × 3 = £27
14 **£224** 7 × 3200 ÷ 100 = 224 or 1% of £3200 is 3200 ÷ 100 = 32, 7% = £32 × 7 = £224
15 **£126** 12.5 × 48 ÷ 100 = 6; so the discount price is £48 − 6 = £42 and three reduced price tickets cost £42 × 3 = £126 or (12.5% is the same as $\frac{1}{8}$ which will be easier to use) $\frac{1}{8}$ × 48 = 6, so $\frac{7}{8}$ = 42. The discount price is £42, so three reduced price tickets cost £42 × 3 = £126
16 **£1.64** 2.5 × 1.60 = 4; £1.60 + £0.04 = £1.64 or 1% × £1.60 = 1.6p, $\frac{1}{2}$% = 0.8p, so $2\frac{1}{2}$% = 1.6 + 1.6 + 0.8 = 4p, so the new price is £1.64.

17 a **£500, B £1000, C £1500** £3000 shared into 6 parts gives £500 per part, so A gets £500, B gets 2 × £500 = £1000, C gets 3 × £500 = £1500

18 **250 ml** $2\frac{1}{2}$ litres = 2500 ml The total number of parts is 2 + 2 + 1 + 5 = 10, each part is therefore $\frac{1}{10}$ of the total, strawberry cordial is one part, so $\frac{1}{10}$ × 2500 = 250 ml

19 a **30 cm**
   b **9 cm** If each 5 m is represented by 2 cm, the length has 75 ÷ 5 = 15 lots of 5 m lengths, which will be represented by 15 × 2 cm = 30 cm; and the width has 22.5 m ÷ 5 = 4.5 lots of 5 m lengths, which will be represented by 4.5 × 2 cm = 9 cm

20 **c** The first letter represents the number of straight lines in the shape (A is 3, B is 4, C is 5). The second letter represents the angles formed by the crossing lines (M has all right angles, N has a mixture of angles). The third letter represents the number of black spots (R is 1, S is 2, T is 3).

21 **b** The first letter represents the shape and position of the shape inside the rectangle (A is a triangle at the top, B is a triangle at the base, C is a semicircle at the top, D is a semicircle at the base). The second letter presents the shading (L is vertical lines, M is black, N is cross-hatched lines).

22 **b** The first letter represents the orientation of the triangle (A has the right angle at the top left, B has it at the bottom left, C has it at the top right). The second letter represents the shape in the corner (D is an x, E is a tick and F is a crescent in a circle). The third letter represents that shading of the circle (X is black, Y is white, Z is a cross).

23 **e** The first letter represents the orientation of the rectangle (A is horizontal, B is vertical). The second letter represents the shapes inside the rectangle (R is a square and a circle, S is two circles, T is two squares). The third letter represents the shading (X is black, Y is white).

24 **133.1 cm** 12.4 m = 124 cm, 55 mm = 5.5 cm, so 124 + 3.6 + 5.5 = 133.1 cm

25 **1 hour 30 minutes 5 seconds** Number of minutes is 5405 ÷ 60 = 90 minutes and 5 seconds, 90 minutes = 1 hour and 30 minutes, so the total is 1 hour 30 minutes 5 seconds.

26 a **Sugar 100 g, butter 150 g, flour 200 g** 2 oz = 50 g so divide by 2 to find 1 oz (50 ÷ 2 = 25); Sugar is 4 g × 25 g = 100 g; butter is 6 g × 25 g = 150 g; flour is 8 g × 25 g = 200 g
   b **0.45 kg** Total weight of ingredients is 100 g + 150 g + 200 g = 450 g = 0.45 kg

27 **00:13** 18 minutes takes 23:42 to midnight which is 00:00 on the 24-hour clock, so another 13 minutes takes it to 00:13.

28 **14:53** 35 minutes before 3.35 p.m. is 3 p.m. and another 7 minutes earlier is 2.53 p.m., which is 14:53 on a digital clock.

29 **10:50** A train travelling at 30 km per hour covers 10 km in 20 minutes. The first train will be halfway between A and B at 10:40. The train leaving B at 10:20 will be a quarter of the way between B and A at 10:40. The distance between the two trains at 10:40 is 10 km, so they will pass after another 5 km each. At 30 km per hour 5 km takes 10 minutes, so they will pass as 10:50.

30 **09:45** $7\frac{1}{2}$ hours after 20:15 is 03:45. The new time zone is 6 hours ahead, so 03:45 plus 6 hours is 09:45.

31 a **E** The line begins and ends at the same weight read off the *y* axis.
   b **A** This is the line that has the greatest difference between the starting and end point on the *y* axis.
   c **B** This is the steepest drop in the line graph from start (birth) to week 1.
   d **A** The line remains horizontal for the first week.

32 50 + 25 + 12 + 23 + 10 = 120 customers; 360° ÷ 120 customers = 3° per person, so multiply the number of customers by 3 each time.

	Number of customers	Angle on pie chart
Beach	50	150 degrees
Mountains	25	75 degrees
Lakeside	12	36 degrees
Cities	23	69 degrees
Theme parks	10	30 degrees

75 degrees 50 beach customers ÷ 2 = 25; 25 × 3° per customer = 75.

Mixed Paper 4

1 **c** The shapes at the top and bottom give the middle shape in the next pattern, which also changes to black. The middle shape gives the top and bottom shape and the horizontal lines are moved to the bottom shape.

2 **c** The number of short horizontal lines in the first shape gives the number of times that a curly line crosses the circle in the second shape; and the small circle at the base of the first shape is repeated at both ends of the curly line with the same shading.

3 **a** The number of sides of the large shape gives the number of rows of smaller shapes. The number of inner black shapes gives the number of times it is repeated at the end of each row and they change to white.

4 **d** The first shape is rotated 180 degrees and the cross is moved to the other end of the L shape. The small white square becomes a white circle.

5 **26 May** Rosie is 13 – 3 days younger that Sara, so Rosie's birthday is 10 days before 5 June, which is 26 May as May has 31 days.

6 **Annie** As Bella and Ellie end up in joint first position, the third person to complete the race is Annie.

7 **365 m** 5 km = 5000 m and 5000 ÷ 5 circuits = 1000 m; 1 width is 135 m so multiply by 2 to find the total of both widths (135 × 2 = 270); then subtract to find the total of both lengths (1000 − 270 = 730) then divide by 2 to find 1 length (730 ÷ 2 = 365)

8 **06:50** The next low tide is at 05:30 + 6 h 20 m = 11:50; the next high tide is 11:50 + 6 h 20 m = 18:10; the next low tide is at 00:30, which will be on Tuesday morning; the next high tide will be at 00:30 + 6 h 20 m = 06:50, the first high tide on Tuesday.

9 a $8\frac{1}{4}$
   b $\frac{23}{5}$ The top number is divided by the bottom number and the remainder is expressed as a fraction.
10 $\frac{1}{4}$ The numerators (top numbers) are multiplied together and the total is divided by the divisors (bottom numbers) multiplied together. So for $\frac{3}{4} \times \frac{1}{2} \times \frac{2}{3}$, $3 \times 1 \times 2 = 6$, $4 \times 2 \times 3 = \frac{6}{21} = \frac{1}{4}$
11 **78** $\frac{1}{4} \times 520 = 130$; $\frac{3}{5} \times 130 = 3 \times 26 = 78$
12 $1\frac{3}{4}$ $\frac{5}{6} + \frac{2}{3} + \frac{1}{4} = \frac{10}{12} + \frac{8}{12} + \frac{3}{12} = \frac{20}{12} = \frac{19}{12} = 1\frac{3}{4}$
13 **a** Each row has one white circle, one black and one with a cross; the inverted L-shape from the top line projects to the right and left alternately; the small square in the top corners alternates between top left and top right.
14 **e** Each row has a repeating pattern made up of four patterns, so along the bottom row the next pattern will have vertical line shading.
15 **d** All of the squares in the grid have a curly line with a black arrowhead and two larger white circles; the number of smaller circles decreases by one along the grid and the crosses increase by one.
16 **b** The four shapes on the outside of the grid are combined in the centre square in the same orientation as they are on the outside; the striped shapes become black, and the black shaded shapes are white in the middle.
17 **d** All of the shapes on the left have two straight lines and one curved line joined end to end with a black circle at either an end or point where two lines join.
18 **a** All of the patterns on the left have five shapes joined in a line with a rhombus (diamond shape) in the centre of the five shapes.
19 **e** All of the patterns on the left are made up of two shapes with half of the larger of the two shapes shaded.
20 **e** All of the patterns on the left have a curly line with three loops and a white circle along the line and a T-line at one end of the line.
21 **63** $(4 \times 3.5) + 7^2 = 14 + (7 \times 7) = 14 + 49 = 63$
22 **126** $35 + (12 \times 3^2) - 17 = 35 + (12 \times 3 \times 3) - 17 = 35 + 108 - 17 = 126$
23 **175** $(10^3 - 5^3) \div 5 = ((10 \times 10 \times 10) - (5 \times 5 \times 5)) \div 5 = (1000 - 125) \div 5 = 875 \div 5 = 175$
24 **13** $(4^2 + 6) - (63 \div 7) = (4 \times 4) + 6) - 9 = 16 + 6 - 9 = 13$
25 **a** rhombus or square
   b kite

26 **a** **8** A hexagon has 6 sides so a hexagonal prism has two hexagonal faces joined by 6 rectangles, giving 8 faces.
   b **18** There are 6 edges round each hexagonal end and 6 edges from one end to the other, making 18 edges.
27 **c** The circle face and the X-face cannot be adjacent, so not option a or e. The arrow cannot point towards the base line of a U-shape, so not b. The square cannot be adjacent to both U-shape faces, so not option d.
28 **e** Cube e cannot be made as the two white circles cannot be adjacent.
29 **e** Cube e cannot be made as the white circle cannot be adjacent to the top of the face with the heart shape.
30 **d** The arrow points to the white circle so cannot point to the black spots or a triangle face, so not options a or b. The two triangles cannot be adjacent, so not option c. The circle and the cross cannot be adjacent, so not option e.
31 **a** **7 cm** Read the measurements carefully off the graph following the grid lines accurately and checking the scale on each axis.
   b **16 cm**
   c **62 cm** $34 + 28 = 62$
   d **5 cm** $8 - 3 = 5$
32 **a** **Mint**
   b Each one of the 40 children will be represented by $\frac{360}{40}$ degrees = 9 degrees, so 12 children will be represented by a sector of **108** degrees.

Curveball Questions 2

1 **a** **9.15 a.m.**
   b **10.45 a.m.** Halfway is 45 km from Alderly and Benton; Mr Stone will reach halfway at 11 a.m. Mr Price is travelling at 60 km per hour which is 1 km per minute, so he will reach the halfway point after 45 minutes. So Mr Price needs to leave at 9.15 a.m. He will arrive at Alderly $1\frac{1}{2}$ hours later, which is 10.45 a.m.
2 **a** **25 minutes** Mother leaves home at 8.40 a.m. for the dance class 20 minutes away that starts at 9.00 a.m., and she is back home by 9.20 a.m. She needs to leave home at 9.45 a.m. to get to the gym class 15 minutes away, so Mother has 25 minutes at home.
   b **20 minutes** It takes 10 minutes to get to the dance class from the gym class. Mother arrives at the gym class at 10 a.m. She needs to get to the dance class for 10.30 a.m., so must leave the gym class at 10.20 a.m. in order to watch the gym class for 20 minutes.
3 The difference between consecutive numbers in the sequence increases by one each time.
   a **BRING FOOD**
   b **4 : 1 : 67 : 67**   **154 : 1 : 79**   **92 : 106 : 191**

A	B	C	D	E	F	G	H	I	J	K	L	M	N	O	P	R	S	T	W
1	2	4	7	**11**	16	22	**29**	37	46	56	**67**	79	92	106	121	**137**	154	172	191
1	2	3	4	**5**	6	7	8	9	10	11	12	13	14	15	16	17	18	19	

Test Paper 1

1. **d** The middle shape in the first pattern gives the outside shape for the second pattern, the small white shapes give the central shape inside the square, and the number of black circles gives the number of crosses in the second pattern.
2. **d** The number of lines in the first shapes gives the number of rows in the second shape, the number of sections in the circle gives the number of circles in the rows with the shading of each section indicating the shading of the circles in each row.
3. **b** The second shape is the first shape rotated 90 degrees clockwise; the long lines are replaced with short lines and the short lines are replaced with long ones; the new long line extends across the base line in the second shape.
4. **e** In the second pattern circles replace the squares, the triangle remains, and all shapes change from black to white or white to black.
5. **2 and 4** $2 \times 6 = 12$, $2 \times 24 = 28$, $2 \times 42 = 84$; $4 \times 3 = 12$, $4 \times 7 = 28$, $4 \times 21 = 84$
6. **33, 49, 81** 33 and 81 are not divisible exactly by 7, and 49 is not divisible exactly by 3
7. **2, 3, 5, 7** These number can only be divided exactly by 1 and themselves – they only have two factors.
8. **White** 10 12 14 16 <u>18</u> – Yellow 20 – Blue 22 – White 24 – Yellow 26 – Blue <u>28 – White</u>
9. **110 litres** After two weeks Doug will have used 14×3 litres = 42 litres; so the tank is down from 150 litres to 108 litres, then 2 litres is added from rain, giving 110 litres in the tank after two weeks.
10. **Toni** Abi's is taller than Harjit's, so it can't be Harjit; Ben's is 5cm taller than Abi's, so it can't be Abi; Ben's is taller than Amy's, so it can't be Amy; if Toni's is 11cm taller than Abi's and Ben's is 5cm taller than Abi's then Toni's must be 6cm taller than Ben's. So Toni's is the tallest.
11. $\frac{3}{16}$ Work out the brackets first: $\frac{3}{4} \times \frac{3}{4} = \frac{9}{16}$; as $\frac{3}{8}$ cannot be simplified, find equivalents of the remaining fractions with denominators of 16 ($\frac{3}{8} = \frac{6}{16}$ and as $\frac{9}{12}$ can be simplified to $\frac{3}{4}$ it is the equivalent of $\frac{12}{16}$); add and subtract the numerators: $9 + 6 - 12 = 3$ so the answer is $\frac{3}{16}$
12. $2\frac{3}{7}$ Find equivalents so all fractions have denominators of 14 ($\frac{5}{7} = \frac{10}{16}$ and as $1\frac{1}{2}$ is $\frac{3}{2}$ this is $\frac{21}{14}$); add the numerators: $10 + 3 + 21 = 34$ so it is $\frac{34}{7}$; divide by 14 to change into a mixed number ($34 \div 14 = 2\frac{6}{14}$ which simplifies to $2\frac{3}{7}$)
13. $3\frac{1}{2}$ $\frac{42}{4} \div \frac{6}{2}$ To divide by a fraction, turn the divisor fraction upside down and multiply first the numerators (top numbers) and then the denominators (bottom numbers). However, before carrying out the multiplications check to see if any of the numbers can be simplified: $\frac{42}{4} \times \frac{2}{6}$ 6 goes into 42 7 times; 2 goes into 4 twice, giving $\frac{7}{2} = 3\frac{1}{2}$
14. $2\frac{1}{4}$ Find equivalents of the fractions with denominators of 12 ($\frac{1}{2} = \frac{6}{12}$; $\frac{1}{4} = \frac{3}{12}$; $\frac{2}{3} = \frac{8}{12}$; and $\frac{5}{6} = \frac{10}{12}$); then add the numerators ($6 + 3 + 8 + 10 = 27$); therefore it is $\frac{27}{12}$ which simplifies to $\frac{9}{4}$ and $2\frac{1}{4}$
15. **114** $40 \times 750 = 30\,000$ and $30\,000 \div 100 = 300$; $30 \times 620 = 186\,000$ and $186\,00 \div 100 = 186$; $300 - 186 = 114$
16. **£390 000** $375\,000 \times 4 = 1\,500\,000$ and $1\,500\,000 \div 100 = 15\,000$; $375\,000 + 15\,000 = 390\,000$
17. **£58 200** $1\,245\,000 - 760\,000 = 485\,000$; $12 \times 485\,000 = 5\,820\,000$ and $5\,820\,000 \div 100 = 58\,200$
18. **d**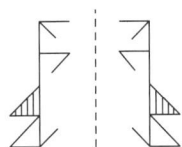
19. **e**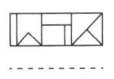

20. **d**
21. **c**
22. **£1160, £2320, £2320, £3480, £4640** The number of parts is $1 + 2 + 2 + 3 + 4 = 12$; the value of each part is £13 920 ÷ 12 = £1160; so portions in the ratio 1 : 2 : 2 : 3 : 4 are £1160, £2320, £2320, £3480, £4640.
23. **3.15 × 4.5** 1m = 2 cm so 0.5 m = 1 cm; $0.5 \times 6.3 = 3.15$ and $0.5 \times 9 = 4.5$. So the actual measurements are 3.15 m × 4.5 m
24. **5.6 kg** Number of parts is $2 + 1 + 4 = 7$; fruit and water make up 3 parts, so 1 part is 4.2 kg ÷ 3 = 1.4 kg, and the weight of the sugar is 1.4 kg × 4 = 5.6 kg
25. **26 years** The total age of 3 uncles is $45 + 53 + 58 = 156$ and their average is $156 \div 3 = 52$. Pascal is half their average $52 \div 2 = 26$
26. a **267.5**
    4280 2140 1070 535 <u>267.5</u>
     ÷2   ÷2   ÷2   ÷2

    b **13.9**
    1.1 4.3 7.5 10.7 <u>13.9</u>
    +3.2 +3.2 +3.2 +3.2
27. **654.0** $10^2 = 100$ and $10^2 = 1000$ So $0.0218 \times 100 = 2.18$; then $2.18 \times 1000 = 2180$; $2180 \times 0.3 = 654.0$
28. $\frac{3}{32}$ All of the others are equivalent to $\frac{1}{8}$.
29. **105** $(8^2 \times 2) + (6^2 - 2^2) - 55 = (64 \times 2) + (36 - 4) - 55 = 128 + 32 - 55 = 105$
30. **83** $4^3 + 3^3 - 2^3 = 4 \times 4 \times 4 + 3 \times 3 \times 3 - 2 \times 2 \times 2 = 64 + 27 - 8 = 83$
31. **1 006 000** $4024 \div 2^2 \times 10^3 = 4024 \div 2 \times 2 \times 10 \times 10 \times 10 = 1006 \times 1000 = 1\,006\,000$

32 **1520** $(5^3 - 7^2) \times 10^2 \div 5 = (5 \times 5 \times 5 - 7 \times 7) \times 10 \times 10 \div 5 = (125 - 49) \times 100 \div 5 = 76 \times 20 = 1520$

33 **4 km 53 m 86.7 cm** 4 053 867 mm = 5386.7 cm = 4053 m 86.7 cm = 4 km 53 m 86.7 cm

34 **1030 kg** 1 ml of water weighs 1 g, then 1 litre weighs 1 kg, and 1000 litres weighs 1000 kg; total weight of the tank is 1000 kg + 30 kg = 1030 kg

35 **B 604 800 s** The hours of one day to minutes: 24 × 60 = 1440; minutes to seconds: 1440 × 60 = 86 400; days to a week: 86 400 × 7 = 604 800

36 **20 cm²** The area of a right angled triangle is $\frac{1}{2} \times$ base × height which is $\frac{1}{2} \times 4 \times 10 = 20$

37 **7000 cm sq** There are two faces with each pair of dimensions: 2 × 30 × 50 = 3000 cm sq; 2 × 30 × 25 = 1500 cm sq; 2 × 25 × 50 = 2500 cm sq. The total area is 3000 + 1500 + 2500 = 7000 m sq
   b 15 slabs Area of patio is (4 × 4) − 1 = 15 sq. m

38 **31 mins** Train A leaves at 09:05 and arrives at 10:10, which is 1 hour 5 mins; train C leaves at 15:45 and arrives 17:21, which is 1 hour 36 mins. The difference between the two is 31 mins.

39 **2 hours 22 mins** The next train to arrive at Beaston (after 14:30) is at 16:52, the difference is 2 hours 22 mins.

40 **Train D** Train A takes 38 mins to get from Acton to Beaston (09:43–09:05); train B takes 54 mins (12:04–11:10); train C takes 1 hour 7 mins (16:52–15:45); train D takes 28 mins (18:38–18:10).

41 **12:50** Train B should arrive at 12:31 at Colbridge, with 14 minutes delay that would become 12:45, and then another 5 minutes delay means the arrival time will be 12:50.

42 a **Trapezium**
   b **Rectangle**
   c **Scalene triangle**
   d **Pentagon**

43 **Triangular-based pyramid**

44 **60 cm** The cuboid has 12 edges, 4 of each length, so total length is (4 × 6) + (4 × 4) + (4 × 5) = 24 + 16 + 20 = 60 cm

45 **North-west** N, then 45 degrees is NE, then 135 degrees is S, then 90 degrees is W, then 45 degrees is NW.

46 **North** Donna sets off facing west, turning left she faces south, then turning right she faces west again, then turning right again she ends up facing north.

47 a **75 degrees** There are 30 degrees between each digit round a clockface, so from 12 to halfway past the two, the small hand has moved 30 + 30 + 15 = 75 degrees
   b **900 degrees** From 12 to 2.30 the big hand has made 2 complete rotations round the clockface and half way round again, which is 360 + 360 + 180 = 900 degrees

48 South-west If ↑ is north, then travel south-west from the harbour to the island.
   Lighthouse   Harbour
              Island

49 a **Tue, Thu, Fri** These are points above the 18°C line
   b **19°C** Average is the total of the five days divided by 5: 15 + 20 + 17 + 23 + 20 = 95, 95 ÷ 5 = 19°C

   c i **7°** 22 − 15 = 7
     ii **10°** 23 − 13 = 10

50 a **73 m** Thinking distance + braking distance is 18 m + 55 m = 73 m
   b **61 m** 75 m − 14 m = 61 m
   c **13 m** At 30 mph the total distance is 9 + 14 = 23 m; at 40 mph it is 12 + 24 = 36 m. The difference is 36 − 23 = 13 m
   d **8** At 20 mph the total is 12 m, at 70 mph it is 96 m, which is 8 times greater than at 20 mph.
   e **40 mph** At 40 mph 2× braking distance is 48 m – anything faster will take a longer distance, so 40 mph is the maximum speed.

51 **15** 17 + 15 + 18 + 13 + 11 + 16 = 91; 90 ÷ 6 = 15

52 **90%** 3 × 86 = 258; 78 + 90 = 168; so the third score must be 258 − 168 = 90

53 a **£91** £56 + £99 + £40 + £140 + £120 = £455, so the average is £455 ÷ 5 = £91
   b **£101** £81 + £99 + £65 + £140 + £120 = £505, average is £505 divided by 5 = £101

54 a **29** 5 × 31 = 155; 4 × 28 = 112; 2 × 27 = 54; 155 + 112 + 54 = 321; number of pupils in twelfth class is 350 − 321 = 29
   b **29** 350 divided by 12 = 29 to the nearest whole number.

55 **£9.85** (3 × £12.50) + (3 × £11) + £28 = £37.50 + £33 + £28 = £98.50, so the average is £98.50 divided by 10 = £9.85

56 **£17** The total cost is 30 × £2.10 = £63; four £20 notes is £80; £80 − £63 = £17

Test Paper 2

1 **460** $0.0023 \times 10^3 \times 200 = 0.0023 \times 1000 \times 200 = 2.3 \times 200 = 460$

2 a **18** 4 6<u>3</u>8 6<u>7</u>4.8<u>4</u>2   3 + 7 + 8 = 18
  b **18** <u>5</u>0 3<u>7</u>6.<u>6</u>73   5 + 7 + 6 = 18

3 **101 011 111**

4 **470**

5 **c** All of the shapes on the left have a white circle in the corner and one of the three shapes shaded black.

6 **d** All of the shapes on the left have a curved line going across the top of a triangle and a circle, with the curved line projecting at each end.

7 **e** All of the shapes on the left are circles with one line across the circle forming a segment with lined shading and another line across the circle extending both ends beyond the circumference with the segment shaded black.

8 **e** All of the shapes on the left are made up of three straight lines with two crossing points, and with circles at three of the ends, two shaded black and one white.

9 **Jit is 37 seconds, Anya is 41 seconds, Matt is 54 seconds** Anya is 7 seconds less than Connor, so Anya is 48 − 7 = 41 seconds; Jit is 4 seconds less than Anya, 41 − 4 = 37 seconds; Matt is 13 seconds slower than Anya, so Matt is 41 seconds + 13 seconds = 54 seconds

10 **7½ mins** 80 litres in 2h, so 40 litres in 1h or 60 mins, and each litre takes $\frac{60}{40} = 1\frac{1}{2}$ minutes, so to replace 5 litres takes $1\frac{1}{2}$ mins × 5 = $7\frac{1}{2}$ minutes

11 **2½ hours** Normally one-quarter of the journey takes one-quarter of the time, which is 30 minutes; with roadworks it takes twice as long. So the total journey time is 1½ hours at usual speed and 1 hour at reduced speed giving a total of 2½ hours.

12 **b** D cannot be colder than B as it is hotter than A, and A is hotter than B.

13 **0.4375** 0.125 × 3.5 = 0.4375 Carry out the long multiplication without decimal points then add the point four places from the right at the end as there are four decimal places together in these two numbers.

14 **863.08** Keep the decimal points in line when doing the addition.

15 **1000** 1101.101 × 5 = 5505.505; the number has been multiplied by 1000 as it has moved three places to the left across the decimal point: 5505.505 × 1000 = 5 505 505

16 **64**

17 **e** Each of the outer squares has a square and circle; the square takes the shading of the circle in the previous circle going back anticlockwise, and the circle has the shading of the square in the adjacent large square moving on one square clockwise; the two black dots are opposite the pair of dots in the central square.

18 **d** A T-shape or inverted T-shape is repeated down each column, the central two columns have black spots going in reverse order in adjacent columns.

19 **d** There is a black circle in the bottom left corner of each outer square, and vertically above the circle is a shape from the central square.

20 **d** The small crosses increase by one down the triangles which have their right angle at the bottom left corner, and the circle shading style is repeated along each diagonal line of triangles.

21 **c** The shape in each corner of the central square is repeated in the outer corner of each outer square of the grid, and the corner squares all have a diagonal lines pointing away from the central square to the outer corners of the grid.

22 **Vicky £8293.75 Rob £24 881.25 Sue £33 175** Each part is $\frac{1}{8}$ of £66 350, and £66 350 ÷ 8 = £8293.75; so Vicky gets £8293.75; Rob gets £8293.75 × 3 = £24 881.25; Sue gets £8293.75 × 4 = £33 175

23 **7 red, 14 white, 21 blue** One part is 42 ÷ 6 = 7, so 2 parts are 14

24 **Cement 1½ kg, coarse sand 6 kg** One part is 3 kg ÷ 2 = 1½ kg, and 4 parts is 6 kg.

25 **5** $3x^2 + 25 = 100$, $3x^2 = 75$, $x^2 = 25$, $x = 5$

26 **a 13** The outer two numbers are multiplied to give the middle number, so 3 × 13 would give 39.
  b 31 The outer two numbers are added together to give the middle number, so 23 + 8 = 31
  c 51 The first number divided by the third number gives the middle number, so as 3 × 17 is 51, 51 ÷ 3 = 17

27 **57** $7^2 + (3 × 2^3) - 4^2$ = 49 + (3 × 2 × 2 × 2) - (4 × 4) = 49 + 24 - 16 = 57

28 **17** $\frac{1}{2}$ × 56 + 108 ÷ 12 − 20 = 28 + (108 ÷ 12) − 20 = 28 + 9 − 20 = 17

29 **139.6** $3490 ÷ 10^2 × 2^2$ = 3490 ÷ (10 × 10) × (2 × 2) = 34.9 × 4 = 139.6

30 **64** $83 + 5 × 9 - 8^2$ = 83 + 45 - (8 × 8) = 128 - 64 = 64

31 **d** The first letter represents the number of circles inside the shape (A is 2, B is 3, C is 4); the second letter represents the outer line style of the shape (D is a single plain line, E is an outer plain and inner dotted line, F is a double plain line, G is a double dotted line); the third letter represents the number of black circles (X is 1, Y is 2, Z is 3).

32 **e** The first letter represents the arrow head at the end of the wavy line (A is a single line, B is a white triangle, C is a black triangle); the second letter represents the number of black spots (X is 2, Y is 3, Z is 1); the third letter represents the position of the wavy line in relation to the two straight lines (P has the wavy line between the straight lines, Q has the wavy line on the outside of the three lines).

33 **c** The first letter represents the shape made by the three plain lines (A is a reversed Z-shape, B is a Z-shape, C is a C-shape, D is a backward facing C-shape); the second letter represents the number of dashed lines across the shape (E has 1, F has 2, G has 3); the third letter represents the shading of the small square (Y has an X, Z is black, X is white).

34 **e** The first letter represents the number of horizontal lines pointing to the right (L is 1, M is 2, N is none). The second letter represents the number of horizontal lines pointing to the left (P is none, Q is 1, R is 2). The third letter represents the number of short horizontal lines at the base of the shape (F is 1, G is 2, H is 3).

35 **360 sq cm** The three different-size faces of the cuboid are 5 cm × 10 cm, 5 cm × 12 cm and 10 cm × 12 cm, and as there are two faces of each size, the four largest faces will be two of 5 × 12 and two of 10 × 12). This gives a total area of the four faces as 120 + 240 = 360 sq cm.

36 **80** Five lengths of 20 cm will fit along the 1 m side with 4 rows (4 × 10 cm) across the side, so one layer is made up of 5 × 4 = 20 bricks. The crate is 40 cm high so it will take four lots of 10 cm or 4 layers, so the total number of bricks is 20 × 4 = 80

37 **112** Divide the area into two rectangles, one is 4 m × 16 m, giving an area of 64 sq m, and the second rectangle will be 6 m × 8 m = 48 sq m, so total area is 64 m + 48 m = 112 sq m

38 **800 m** $\frac{1}{4}$ of the distance is 1200 m, then the total distance in 1200 m × 4 m = 4800 m; the track is hexagonal with 6 sides, so each side is 4800 m ÷ 6 m = 800 m long

39 **2¼ hours** 60 miles in 1 hour, 120 miles in 2 hours, and 15 miles will take quarter of an hour, so the total time is 2¼ hours.

40

	Quarter past midnight	4.55am	midday	3.30pm	9.45pm	Ten to midnight
24-hour clock	00:15	04:55	12:00	15:30	21:45	23:50

41 **9.10 a.m.** 7.10 a.m. plus 17 minutes plus 1 hour 42 minutes = 9.10 a.m.
42 **11 580 mins** 1 week is 7 days, and 1 day has 24 hours, so 8 days has 8 × 24 hours = 192 hours, plus an extra hour is 193 hours. Each hour has 60 mins, so the total number of minutes is 193 × 60 = 11 580 mins
43 a **63°** There are 180 degrees in a triangle, and the base angles of an isosceles triangle are equal, so 180 − 54 = 126, $\frac{1}{2}$ × 126 = 63 degrees
   b **ABF is a scalene triangle, CDE is an isosceles triangle**
44 **4 pairs of parallel lines**
45 a **12 straight**
   b **6 straight**
   c **2 curved**
   d **1 curved**
46 **d** The arrow cannot point to the white circle.
47 **d** The black circle cannot be adjacent to the face with the X.
48 **c** The arrow needs to point to the white circle, so it cannot be a; the black triangle cannot be adjacent to the white circle, so it is not b; the white triangle cannot be adjacent to the black circle, so it is not d; and the arrow cannot be adjacent to the diagonal line shading, so it is not e.
49 **e** The arrow needs to point to the white triangle, so it is not a; the arrow and the black triangle cannot be adjacent, so it is not b; the @ cannot be adjacent to the line shading, so it is not c or d.
50 a **85 balloons** The total is 18 + 20 + 11 + 15 + 23 + 8 = 85
   b **12 more yellow than orange** 23 − 11 = 12
   c **4 orange and 7 purple** Orange 15 − 11 = 4; purple 15 − 8 = 7
   d **Green** Blue is 20, 20 − 5 = 15, there are 15 green balloons.
51 a **6**
   b **$\frac{1}{3}$** Total vehicles is 48 + 30 + 36 + 12 + 18 = 144, cars were $\frac{48}{114} = \frac{4}{12} = \frac{1}{3}$
   c **12** 36 vans, $\frac{1}{3}$ × 36 = 12
52 a

   b i **11** 53 − 42 = 11
     ii **28** 38 − 10 = 28
53 a **74** Each 1% represents 2 people, so 2 × 37 = 74
   b **location** Responses range from grade 1 to grade 5.
   c **choice of topics** 54% after quality of refreshments with 82%.
   d **14** 37% for better grades and 30% poorer grade for location, so the difference is 7% which represents 14 people.
54 a **May** Rainfall is 129 mm
   b **53 mm** The wettest is 129 mm, the driest is 76 mm, the difference is 129 mm − 76 mm = 53 mm
   c **16.2°** The total of the three months is 22.2 + 6.4 + 10 = 48.6, so the average is 48.6 divided by 3, which is 16.2.
   d **24.7°** 27.5° is the hottest and 2.8° is the coolest, the difference is 27.5 − 2.8 = 24.7.
   e **Jun/Jul and Jul/Aug** June 25.6° to July 27.5° is less than 2°; July 27.5° to Aug 26.1° is less than 2°.
55 7 + 2 + 9 + 3 + 5 + 4 = 30 and 360° ÷ 30 = 12° per person, so multiply each number by 12

	Yellow	Orange	Red	Purple	Blue	Green
	7	2	9	3	5	4
No. of degrees on pie chart	84	24	108	36	60	48

   b **Purple 60°, Red 132°** Purple goes from 3 to 5, so the angle will be 5 × 12 = 60 degrees; red goes from 9 to 11, so the angle will be 11 × 12 = 132 degrees

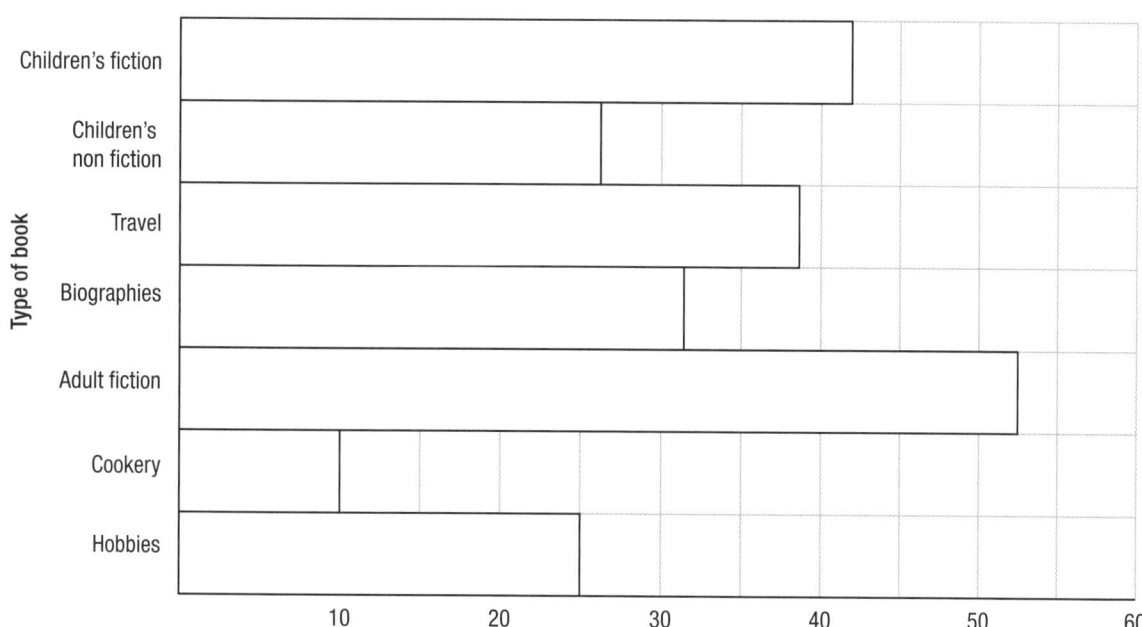

Notes